WHEN WORK EQUALS LIFE:

The Next Stage of Workplace Violence

BY

S. Anthony Baron, Ph.D.,Psy.D.
Suzanne J. Hoffman, Ph.D.
James G. Merrill, SPHR

NEW ENGLAND INSTITUTE
OF TECHNOLOGY
LEARNING RESOURCES CENTER

Published By:
Pathfinder Publishing of California
3600 Harbor Blvd.
Oxnard, CA 93035

1

5- 01   # 44752839

WHEN WORK EQUALS LIFE

Published By
Pathfinder Publishing of California
3600 Harbor Blvd., # 82
Oxnard, CA 93035, U.S.A.

Copyright 2000 by S. Anthony Baron, Suzanne J. Hoffman, and James G. Merrill

No Part of this book may be reproduced or transmitted in any form or by any means, electronic or mechanical, including photocopying, recording or by any information storage and retrieval system without written permission from the authors, except for the inclusion of brief quotations in a review

Pathfinder Publishing of California
3600 Harbor Boulevard, # 82
Oxnard, CA 93035
(805) 984-7756

Library of Congress Cataloging-in Publication Data S. Anthony Baron
When Work Equals Life, The next Stage Of Work Place Violence / by S. Anthony Baron, Suzanne Hoffman, and James G. Merrill
p. cm
Includes bibliographical references
ISBN 0-934793-66-2
1. Violence - United States. 2. Violence - United States - Prevention.

Acknowledgements

The authors would like to acknowledge the following individuals for their assistance and support in producing this book. Lois M. Kosch, Esq. of Wilson, Petty, Kosmo and Turner and Christopher Martin, Esq. of Gibson, Dunn and Crutcher LLP for their input on legal issues; Hal Goudarzi of Goudarzi Investigations and Robert Bauder of United Defense LP for adding their expertise to the chapter on security issues; and Roberta Baron of Baron Center, Inc. for her editorial assistance. We would also like to thank Muriel Housman for her administrative support during the course of this project.

This book is written in memory of all the victims of workplace violence.

Dedications

To Bobbi Baron, my wife, my partner and friend for life. She exemplifies the true spirit of peace, love and truth. Without her commitment to the mission of safety and harmony in the workplace and her devotion to help those in need, Baron Center, Inc. would not be what it is today. It is to her that this book is dedicated. -AB

This book is also dedicated to Robert Hoffman, whose love, support and encouragement made the completion of this book possible. -SH

Table Of Contents

Contents

6

Contents

Early Intervention
Dealing with the Emotionally Enraged Individual
Crisis Procedures

8

WHEN WORK EQUALS LIFE

THE NEXT STAGE IN WORK-PLACE VIOLENCE

BY

S. Anthony Baron, Ph.D.,Psy.D.
Suzanne J. Hoffman, Ph.D.
James G. Merrill, SPHR

Published By:
Pathfinder Publishing of California
3600 Harbor Blvd. # 82
Oxnard, CA 93035

Introduction

On June 9, 1997 a Department of Defense employee walked into the Monterey Presidio Logistical Support Center and began firing a .22 semi-automatic rifle. The assailant, computer specialist John Filler, age 46, wounded one victim and killed another. Following his arrest Filler told police, "I was the one. I did it" and described his actions as a "premeditated ambush."

A fired employee returned to his former workplace, Yaanimax, Inc., on June 13, 1997 with a gun and killed a female co-worker and severely wounded his old boss at an embroidery factory in Santa Fe Springs, California. The gunman used a .38-caliber weapon on both his victims, fled the scene, and then turned the gun on himself a short time later. The assailant had been laid off approximately six weeks prior to the shooting, and was reportedly a former business partner of the victims. This incident occurred just eight days after another fatal workplace shooting at a nearby plastics factory in which an employee killed two co-workers and injured four others before killing himself.

On September 4, 1997, Jesus Antonio Tamayo, a postal worker, shot and critically injured his former wife and her female friend as they stood in line inside a crowded post office, then stepped outside and shot himself. Tamayo, a 64-year old man who had been employed for 21 years with the U.S. Postal Service, was working alone when he saw his former wife enter the post office. Witnesses state that upon seeing his ex-wife, he went to his car and returned with a gun. Both women were shot in the abdomen. Detectives stated that it was unclear what kind of problems the gunman had with his ex-wife, from whom he had been divorced for four and a half years.

When Work Equals Life: The Next Stage of Workplace Violence is a hands-on guide designed to assist employers and managers/supervisors in understanding the ingredients which are thought to have caused violence to occur in the workplace; the profiles and warning signs of potentially violent employees; organizational factors which contribute to workplace violence; and more importantly, the systems, policies and processes organizations need to implement to reduce the risks of violence. This book was written by experts who have had hands-on experience in making organizations effective in dealing with this serious problem. Its purpose is to provide the readers, whether they be management, human resources, executive or front-line employees, valuable knowledge regarding this serious workplace issue as well as the tools to address potentially violent situations and implement practical interventions and solutions.

Who Should Read This Book?
- CEOs (Chief Executive Officers) and Key Executives
- Human Resources Vice Presidents and Managers
- Employee Assistance Program (EAP) Professionals
- Managers and Supervisors
- Safety & Risk Management Professionals
- Legal Professionals
- Security Professionals
- Labor Relations & Union Officials
- Concerned Employees

Along with the tragic increase in workplace violence, leaders in the field have provided greater insight into the causes of this growing menace. When Work Equals Life: The Next Stage of Workplace Violence will provide not only a clearer understanding of the ingredients which contribute to these catastrophic events, but will also provide suggestions and tools to become organizationally effective in reducing the risks of violence.

Through real case histories, ways in which concerned individuals can take effective action to defuse and reduce the risks

Introduction

of a potentially violent employee carrying out a devastating plan will be illustrated. Additionally, sample policies and procedures will be provided; these policies are models that can be put in place immediately in any organization to commence an effective prevention program to protect employees.

It is our greatest hope that, with education, guidance and intervention at the pre-hire, post-hire and even post-trauma levels, violence in the workplace can be addressed in a direct and prophylactic manner. We strongly believe that only through involving employees at all levels of an organization in an effective workplace violence prevention program will this growing tide of violence secede.

Test Your Knowledge

As you begin the process of using this book to increase your knowledge and expertise about the issue of workplace violence, this quiz is offered as a "self-assessment" of your current understanding of the problems faced by many employers in addressing threats and aggression in organizations. The answers can be found in APPENDIX C.

True or False:

1. There is no need to worry about workplace violence because the number of reported homicides at work is decreasing. **T F**

2. All verbal threats should be reported and investigated since this is a form of violence. **T F**

3. Internal violence usually comes from customers, vendors and members of the public. **T F**

4. There is no way to tell if someone has the potential to become violent. **T F**

5. All employees who have verbalized threats should be terminated immediately. **T F**

6. Employee Assistance Programs (EAP) can be useful in preventing workplace violence. **T F**

7. When an incident of workplace violence occurs, the responsibility for the incident lies with the individual, and not with the organization itself. **T F**

8. Effective pre-employment screening, including the use of

background checks on new employees, can effectively reduce violence. **T F**

9. The purpose of a Threat Assessment Team is to determine whether or not an individual will commit an act of violence. **T F**

10. Fitness-for-duty evaluations can be done by any licensed medical or mental health professional. **T F**

11. Training staff, supervisors and managers is one of the less effective methods of implementing a violence prevention program in an organization. **T F**

12. Security systems tend to be not very effective in situations where the person making the threat is an employee, because the employee typically has access to the facility anyway. T F

13. Workplace Violence policies should include a statement about "limited tolerance." **T F**

14. An employer cannot get into trouble for keeping an employee that it suspects may be capable of violence. **T F**

15. Type II violence includes domestic violence incidents. **T F**

Chapter One
The Growing Problem

Workplace Violence continues to be a major concern. The problem will not disappear without proactive and aggressive intervention by organizations.

Allen Halcrow, Editor in Chief of The Personnel Journal, has written an editorial, which begins:

> "On my desk right now, inches from the picture of my smiling 2 year-old niece, is a photocopy of a death certificate. It reduces the life of a 29-year-old woman to nothing more than minor details: her address, her social security number, and her job title. In the middle of the page, under "Immediate Cause," someone has stated dispassionately, "Multiple gunshot wounds."

> The individual was murdered at her desk on August 23, 1993. After killing her, her assailant - a co-worker - shot and killed himself in the same office. How could this tragedy have been avoided? Her family and co-workers continue to ask why this happened."

Violence in the workplace in recent years has grown to

be the second leading cause of death in the workplace, transportation accidents are number one. In 1993, an estimated 1,063 individuals were killed in job related homicides, compared with 6,271 total fatal occupational injuries. In 1994, the number of workplace homicides rose to 1,321. Startlingly, homicide is now the leading cause of death for women in the workplace. Additionally, approximately one-sixth of women murdered in the workplace in 1996 were killed by a husband, boyfriend or relative (National Census of Fatal Occupational Injuries, 1996). Although violence can occur in any occupational setting, those occupations most associated with workplace assault and homicide are in the public service industry and include taxicab drivers, convenience store personnel and food service workers.

General Statistics Regarding the Incidence and Prevalence of Workplace Violence:

- 1980's: U.S. averaged 760 on-the-job murders per year

- 1990's: U.S. averaging about 1000 - 1600 workplace homicides per year

- The workplace is one of the nation's <u>fastest growing</u> murder sites

- An estimated two-million workers are physically attacked each year

- Homicide is currently the leading cause of workplace death for women

- In 1992 there were approximately 6,000 workplace fatalities overall, of which there were approximately 1,000 workplace homicides. Of these, 50 were killed by co-workers and 50 were killed by spouses

- In 1996 there were 6,112 workplace fatalities overall; 1,144 were workplace assaults/injuries and 912 resulted in Workplace Homicides.

Even though the general statistics are staggering, the relevant percentage of workplace homicides involving co-workers or spouses is small. However, these incidents continue to occur. Organizations now face the unsettling problem of never knowing when or where these devastating events will happen.

Of note is the fact that following a five-year high in the occurrence of workplace homicide in 1994, the homicide rate fell 16% below this rate in 1996. While most industries had declines in the number of job-related homicides in 1996, the retail trade and services category had slight increases during 1995. Managers of food serving and lodging establishments, and sales supervisors and proprietors, were particularly affected by the increases. Taxicab drivers, while still one of the most at-risk groups for homicide on the job, had the largest decline in homicides in 1996 (National Census of Fatal Occupational Injuries, 1996).

Speculation about the reasons for decrease in work-related homicide includes increased awareness in recent years about this growing problem and increased security measures including pre-employment testing, background checks and the use of video and surveillance. The implementation of termination interviews and procedures, specialized education and training regarding workplace violence, and most importantly, the implementation of specific workplace violence policies and procedures are also likely contributors to the reduction of workplace homicide.

Although statistics show that workplace murders may never occur in 95% of our organizations this year, they show no selective environmental pattern, particularly with regard to violent acts committed by co-workers and spouses. Thus, all organizations must be prepared to identify potentially violent employees and correct environmental factors that can contribute to the likelihood of a violent incident. In essence, they must acknowledge the possibility of such a potential disaster. To gamble that "it won't happen here" is no longer an acceptable position for any company to adopt. Employees rely on safe working environments. They deserve, and can legally expect, no less.

Types of Workplace Violence

When the circumstances under which workplace assaults occur is examined, three major types of violence appear predominant. The State of California Department of Industrial Relations, Division of Occupational Safety and Health (Cal/OSHA) identifies these three types by the relationship that the perpetrator has to the affected workplace. Some occupations and workplaces will be at risk for more than one of these types of assault. In all three types of these workplace violence incidents, a human being or "hazardous agent" commits the assault (Cal/OSHA Guidelines for Security, 1995).

Type I – The perpetrator has no legitimate business relationship to the workplace and usually enters the workplace to commit a robbery or other criminal act. An example of Type I violence might be an individual who holds up a bank and shoots a teller or a perpetrator who robs a taxicab driver at gunpoint.

Type II – In this type of violence, the perpetrator is either the recipient or the object of a service provided by the affected workplace or victim. For example, the assailant is a current or former client, patient, customer, passenger, criminal suspect, inmate or prisoner. Examples of Type II violence are the irate customer who is upset with his bill and physically attacks a receptionist, or a medical patient who is dissatisfied with her HMO and threatens a claims processor with bodily harm.

Type III – This is the type of violence that occurs least frequently, and yet receives the most media attention. In Type III workplace violence, the perpetrator has some employment-related involvement with the affected workplace. Usually this involves assault by a current or former employee, supervisor or manager, by a current/former spouse or lover, a relative or friend, or some other person who has a dispute with an employee of the affected workplace (Cal/OSHA Guidelines for Security, 1995). A disgruntled or terminated employee looking for revenge is a typical case of Type III violence.

The majority of workplace homicides (approximately 60%-75% depending upon which state) involve a person entering a late-night retail establishment, i.e., liquor store, gas station or convenience store, to commit a robbery. During the commission of the robbery, an employee or the proprietor is injured or killed. Individuals who work late at night and/or early into the morning, and who work alone, are at the greatest risk for this type of violence. Type II violence is on the rise for individuals who provide services to the public, i.e., public sector employees. Increasing concern related to the prevalence of Type II violence is also evident for those who are medical, mental health, social welfare, teaching, law enforcement and justice system professionals. Type III events, while accounting for the smallest number of actual workplace fatalities, often attract the largest amount of media attention. In fact, the media attention that these events receive results in Type III events appearing to be much more common than they actually are (Cal/OSHA Guidelines for Security, 1995). Typical targets of Type III violence are managers and supervisors, or co-workers. In increasing numbers, Type III events are involving romantic and domestic violence in which an employee is threatened in the workplace by an individual with whom they have a personal relationship outside of the workplace.

Current statistics estimate that 70% of domestic violence victims are employed, and over 70% of those victims report that the abusers harass them while they are at work, either over the telephone or in person. These types of incidents account for, in large part, the great number of homicides involving women in the workplace.

Current data related to the number of non-fatal assaults at work is incomplete, and difficult to estimate. However, it appears that the number of assaults that happen at work which result in injury, but are non-fatal, far exceed the number of Type III fatal events. The Bureau of Justice Statistics, in a special report on workplace violence from 1992-1996, estimated that during that period of time more than 2 million U.S. residents were the victims of a violent crime while they were at work or on duty. About 40% of the victims of non-fatal violent incidents in this study reported that they knew their offenders. Some of the most prevalent Type III incidents involve threats, verbal harassment and the sabotage of personal and company property. These are incidents that are often not reported or even thought of as "workplace violence."

For the purposes of this book, we will be focusing primarily on Type III violence, or violence which occurs within the context of an employment relationship.

Workplace Violence Is More Than Homicide

The most famous and most publicized cases of workplace violence are those in which homicide has occurred, particularly those that were committed by co-workers or another individual with whom the victim was acquainted. However, workplace violence does not just include incidents in which one or more persons was seriously injured or killed. Workplace violence can also include verbal aggression, belligerence, sexual harassment, destruction of workplace property, sending violent or threatening messages via notes or e-mail and recurrent physical fights. These behaviors, while receiving less media attention than workplace homicide, nonetheless, are more frequent, pervasive and sometimes destructive to those within the organizational environment. Baron (1993) described workplace violence in terms of three levels of behavior:

Level One:
- Refusal to cooperate with immediate supervisor
- Spreads rumors and gossip to hurt others
- Consistently argues with co-workers
- Belligerent toward customers and clients
- Constantly swears at others
- Makes unwanted sexual comments

Level Two:
- Argues increasingly with co-workers, vendors, customers and management
- Refuses to obey company policies and procedures
- Sabotages equipment and steals company property for revenge
- Verbalizes wish to hurt co-workers and/or management
- Sends sexual or violent notes to co-workers and/or management
- Views self as victimized by management

Level Three:
- Recurrent suicidal and/or homicidal threats
- Recurrent physical fights
- Destruction of property
- Utilization of weapons to harm others
- Commission of murder, rape, arson

Level One and Level Two violence are often dismissed or trivialized by co-workers and supervisors. Comments like, "that's just Dan – he has a short fuse" or "just ignore Lori's dramatic behavior and it will go away" are not uncommon. The reality is that Level One and Level Two violence left unchecked can develop into Level Three types of violence. We need to approach problems while they are small. Recognizing early warning signs of trouble and addressing behavioral issues at incubation stages, rather than waiting until an employee poses a significant threat to another worker or the organization as a whole, are very important steps that should be taken to prevent potential tragedies.

The Costs of Workplace Violence

The costs, financially, emotionally and organizationally, of workplace violence can be staggering. A study by the Safe Workplace Institute put the annual cost of occupational violence to American businesses at $4.2 billion. The same study found that in 1992, there were 11,000 "serious" incidents that cost employers $250,000 per incident; 30,000 "medium" severity incidents cost employers an average of $30,000, while 70,000 "lower" severity incidents cost employers an average of $10,000 per incident. The costs involved are related to four major areas: loss of productivity, employee turnover and associated costs, litigation and legal fees, and other costs related to occurrence (1994, Workplace Violence Research Institute).

Examples of Post-Trauma Costs to Organizations:
During the first 12 months following workplace homicide (Source: Baron, 1993):

Elgar Corporation	$ 400,000.00
General Dynamics	$ 1,200,000.00
Pettit and Martin	$ 1,300,000.00

The Problem

(law firm no longer in existence in San Francisco)
Employment Development Department- $2,000,000.00
two locations, one perpetrator
  (Oxnard and Ventura, California)
United States Postal Service - $250,000.00*
two different incidents, same day (Dearborn, Michigan and Dana Point, California)

*First 24 Hours

    The greatest measurable costs in terms of decreased productivity are most likely to occur during the first week following the violent incident (1994, Workplace Violence Research Institute). Losses are caused most frequently by the absence of those who are injured or killed, work interruptions caused by investigations and media coverage, and interruptions due to damaged equipment. Loss of productivity is also manifested in the psychological responses of workers to the incident. Work time is spent discussing the incident with co-workers and in on-site or off-site counseling sessions. Depression and post-traumatic stress disorder following an incident can also result in poor concentration and distractibility, which impact job performance (1994, Workplace Violence Research Institute).

    Significantly increased rates of employee turnover are also associated with incidents of workplace violence. Following a violent incident, employees can experience a variety of emotions toward their employer. These include feelings of betrayal, anger, guilt and vulnerability. What was once a safe environment is now a dangerous place. For some employees, returning to a place where they witnessed or experienced a violent crime becomes difficult or impossible. Loyalty to the organization is compromised, and the employee begins to look for ways to leave the job. The costs of recruiting and retraining new employees to replace those who leave their positions following a violent incident

23

is almost always an expensive process (1994, Workplace Violence Research Institute).

Litigation and legal fees following an incident of workplace violence represent a considerable portion of the quantifiable expenses associated with workplace violence. Multiple lawsuits following a workplace homicide are common, and are usually against the corporation where the incident took place. Negligent hiring, supervision and/or termination are often listed as cause for the lawsuits. Most of these lawsuits are settled out of court. While many of these types of cases are covered by insurance, substantial deductibles, insurance limits and costs such as lawsuit defense contribute to the skyrocketing legal bills associated following a serious violent incident.

Other quantifiable expenses can include building repair and clean-up, lost wages, property damage, theft, employee turnover, increased security and insurance costs and the medical and psychological treatment associated with a violent incident. Some organizations never recover financially and eventually close their doors forever.

Finally, what may be most difficult to measure directly are the emotional and psychological costs, which also have a very palpable effect on organizational climate, efficiency and ultimately profitability of the company in which an incident of workplace violence has occurred. These psychological sequelae can include depression, post-traumatic stress disorder and anxiety disorders. Finally, the impact of negative media coverage and diminished image in the eyes of customers and the public at large, while difficult to measure, are likely to constitute a significant financial impact for any organization.

Case Study: A Near Tragedy
The following is a true story, one that will be revisited in

this book, as the causes of violence occurring in the workplace are discussed and as the solutions to this growing problem are explored.

Early one day in March 1999, Mark, a machine operator for a large company, arrived at work. About one hour into his shift, Mark began to show signs of nervousness. He walked into the office of his supervisor, Joan, and asked to be allowed to take the day off on leave. Joan checked the schedule and workload and told Mark that he was needed to work that day, as there was no one to replace him on his machine.

Mark became more obviously upset, due to the build-up of emotional pressures he had been experiencing. He told Joan that if he were not given leave, he would go home sick. At that point, Joan told him that if he went home sick, she would require medical documentation upon his return. Mark, feeling a flood of emotions overtake him, began to lose control of his temper. Admittedly, he had always had some difficulty taking direction from Joan, and became very angry and upset with her directive. Previous to this incident, he had never been told that he was an absence abuser, in which case he would have been required to show the requested documentation. He began to assume that Joan was singling him out unfairly. Joan's supervisor, Bob, had previously counseled Mark following a 14-day suspension in February for disruptive behavior. At that time Bob told Mark that, if he ever felt the need to vent his emotions on the workroom floor, he should instead come to Bob's office and express himself privately. So, Mark decided to find Bob. He did not ask for permission to do so.

Mark went to Bob's office, but could not find him. He was becoming even more upset, beginning to hyperventilate and cry. He finally found Bob in a hallway, talking with two other supervisors. Mark exploded at the scene, throwing his lunch

Chapter 1

bucket into a wall. He screamed at the men, "If you don't take care of that bitch, I will." He yelled that, if nothing were done on his behalf, he wouldn't be held accountable for his actions. He was completely out of control. Bob had never seen anyone that angry on the job, and became fearful for Joan's life and safety, as well as his own. He took Mark to his office, left, and returned with two shop stewards. After some discussion, Bob sent Mark home on leave, advising him to seek medical help. He also notified Mark that he would be hearing from the company.

After conducting an investigation, the company sent Mark a letter of discharge dated April 30, 1999, labeled "For Disruptive Behavior and Verbal Abuse," citing the incident with Joan. The letter included mention of three prior disciplinary actions taken over the past three years for similar behavior. The letter was mailed with a certified return receipt.

About two weeks later, the company received the following letter from Mark's brother-in-law: "It was a weekday in May 1999. My sister called me in distress and told me that Mark was going to kill his supervisor and whoever else got in his way. I was afraid for my sister, and for what was about to take place, so I drove to their home."

"As I entered the driveway, my sister met me outside and appeared scared and deeply concerned. I asked about Mark; she told me that he was in the woods and was armed. We went inside and were discussing the situation when Mark walked in the patio doors. I was shocked to see him. He was in Vietnam fatigues, a hat to match, armed belt across his chest, a rifle strapped to his shoulder and side arm, and a knife on his other side. It was a frightening situation. He greeted me and proceeded to tell me his intentions. He was very angry, nervous, and very set on his decision. He was waiting for his supervisor's shift to start and kept checking his watch. I convinced him to sit and talk

to me. He told me that he was tired of fighting the company."

"He appeared to be a man giving up on life. His intention was to commit suicide after his completed plot. After an hour of pleading with him and discussing the situation, I convinced him to allow me to try and help him. I told him of my plan to seek help or counseling for him. I was desperate and didn't know what else to come up with."

There is no doubt that if it had not been for Mark's brother-in-law, Mark would have played out his plan to kill Joan and perhaps other employees as well.

As the individual and organizational ingredients that lead to violence in the workplace are discussed, Mark's case will illustrate a real life experience from which to work, providing both insight into the origins of these problems as well as a framework in which to explore the range of solutions and interventions to this problem.

DISCUSSION QUESTIONS:

1.   It is clear that workplace violence is not a fad, but a reality that will not go away. Based on the author's comments, discuss what you see as the primary components to workplace aggression in today's worksites.

2.   According to OSHA, there are three types of workplace violence. What type does your company or organization primarily have to deal with at work?

3.   Discuss the reasons why organizations have a tendency to ignore Level One aggression at the worksite. What is your organization doing about Level One?

Chapter 1

4.   Most organizations have a "Mark" in their workforce. Discuss what are your natural tendencies with people like "Mark." How would your organization respond to Mark?

Chapter Two
Ingredients for Workplace Violence

Unless the potential causes of workplace violence are understood, solutions cannot be developed. This portion of the book focuses on a number of factors which, when combined, point to a high potentiality for violence. The good news is that, once factors which cause these catastrophic events are elucidated, organizational effectiveness to minimize their occurrence can be established and correspondingly the potential to de-escalate a threatening situation before it becomes a critical incident is increased.

As any chemist knows, when certain chemicals are mixed, a violent reaction will occur. However, if one component of the formula is excluded, the chemical reaction will be aborted. The following chapters outline those ingredients that have caused such havoc in the workplace.

I. A Violent Society,
The Media & the "Copy Cat" Mentality

Americans live in a society where media function almost without restraint, seemingly heedless of its impact. There is no question that what we read, listen to, and see on a daily basis, influences behavior. One cannot pick up a newspaper or turn on a television news program that does not contain some article about the upsurge of violence occurring in our homes, in our streets, with our youth, and in our offices and corporations. Although we appreciate our treasured freedoms of speech and the press, we must realize that the "bad news" syndrome has and will continue to influence behavior. Readers will get ideas from the printed word and stories which have been broadcast. Role models for violent and aggressive behavior are offered in films and on television. People have, and will continue to, mirror events as long as those events are published, portrayed in news reports, movies, video games and sporting events, to name a few. The reality is that we live in an environment that models and reinforces brutality, both real and fictitious. Ultimately, the cost to our society is that we become desensitized to and even normalize the violent images we are inundated with on a daily basis.

> ➤ **TV & Movies -** How many times in a day do you suppose violent acts are displayed on television? It's often been observed that a picture is worth a thousand words; the images of violent acts on television and in the movies also reinforce violent behavior. Those violent images desensitize the population to real violence. Young people have become much more tolerant of violence as a daily event than the youth of just ten years ago. The UCLA Television Monitoring Report and MediaScope, Inc. have played an important role in assessing violence in television. Recent studies have found that television shows containing violent scenes rose from slightly over half of the prime-time programming in October 1994 to about two-thirds in June, 1997. Nearly 40 % of the violent incidents in the study were initiated by "good" characters likely to be perceived as role-attractive models while only 15 % of the programs showed the long-term negative consequences of violence. Perpetrators go unpunished in 73% of all violent scenes. One out of four violent interactions viewed on cable television involves the use of handguns. Presently, it

appears that the risks of viewing the most common depictions of televised violence include learning to behave violently, becoming more desensitized to the harmful consequences of violence, and becoming more fearful of violent attacks.

➢ **Tolerance Level** - Over the years, the tolerance level regarding violence has increased, and many factors have contributed to its rise. The media, movies, and television depict violence thousands of times each day, and our organizations tolerate both major and minor threats, fights, and simple mistreatment between people. Our youth regard violence as part of the American social fabric. Shootings in the streets, domestic violence and child abuse are witnessed by many with indifference. The number of fights in our professional sports has increased also over the years. These athletes are considered "role models," so what is the effectual message? Violence in our society has in effect become "normalized." Violent behavior is consistently portrayed as an acceptable and even glamorous way to resolve differences, "settle scores" and demonstrate power and control.

➢ **Economic, Social and Employment Factors** – Kinney and Johnson (1993) proposed that there may be four social/environmental control processes which are known to discourage violent behavior. These are: an efficient economy, high levels of employment, an effective legal system and a cultural system that maintains norms for good behavior. In the United States in the late twentieth century, we tend to have moderate to high rates of unemployment, an overburdened and inefficient criminal justice system and a popular culture that glamorizes violence and offers competing and often confusing models of acceptable behavior. Further, when threats to job security are perceived, and unemployment becomes a reality, aggression often becomes a "last ditch" effort to exert control over a very frightening and uncertain future.

Taken together, it is clear that the models of violence presented to us, both real and fictitious, in news stories, movies, on television and depicted by sports heroes and others in the media spotlight, promote the normalization of violence in our culture today. It is this progressive desensitization to violence that makes violent options to dispute resolution an increasingly acceptable and even routine process in all arenas of society, including the workplace.

II. Access to, and Knowledge, of Weapons
The availability, accessibility and acceptability of firearms in our culture today help create an environment in which deadly violence is an option for settling disputes. The time in which weapons were used primarily for hunting and protection are gone. Guns are glamorized and portrayed as necessary and even chic accessories for individuals today. Additionally, the right to own a weapon has become a political issue for many, and the safety and societal issues involved in allowing people to own guns are often overridden by political concerns and historical precedents.

➢ **Constitutional Right to Bear Arms** - The founding fathers did not foresee an intended right in our constitution for citizens to own and use AK-47s against each other. Neither could they have envisioned a day in which citizens would have more firepower than the police, who are charged with the responsibility to protect them. Many individuals feel very strongly about their right to own a weapon, and as a free society, we have been limited in our ability to prohibit individuals from owning weapons, including guns. The result is that these weapons are more often used as methods of offensive violence rather than defensive, which was our forefathers' original intention.

➤ **Gun Lobby** - The gun lobby, which has a right to express its views, has been a major factor in preventing the government from dealing effectively with the escalation of assault weapons. As a result, these weapons are regularly landing in the hands of the mass population with ease of accessibility. The necessity of utilizing background checks, including criminal histories, before issuing firearm permits, is an issue that has been debated and argued for years in state legislatures. Even for those who have not been approved for licensure to own a firearm, the availability of guns, including assault weapons, on the black market has increased significantly in recent years.

➤ **Expert Knowledge** - The Vietnam War caused many social problems for those who participated in, and were impacted by, the horrors of that conflict. One of the outputs was the expert firearm knowledge that many gained during that era. In addition, many of the people who have perpetrated serious or fatal acts of workplace violence have been obsessed with the collection and expert use of weaponry. Para-military groups such as neo-nazis, skinheads and white supremacy groups have prided themselves on their accumulation of dangerous and lethal weapons, as well as on the knowledge and ability to use them. Together, this can be a dangerous recipe for violence anywhere, including the work environment.

III. Mental Illness

In all cases, mental illness has been a core factor for those who commit workplace homicides. Most mentally ill persons are not dangerous. However, a small percentage of those who are mentally ill, who are not under effective treatment, are capable of killing their co-workers, supervisors, or spouses. We have honored their request for anonymity, but an internal study by one Fortune 100 organization showed a 98% correlation between those employees who made threats and their impaired mental states. Diagnoses of those employees ranged from disordered personality to schizophrenia. Again and again as these cases are reviewed, the following psychological characteristics are observed, almost without exception.

> **Depression**

Clinical depression is the most common presenting problem seen by therapists, counselors and psychologists. While everyone has days where they "have the blues," feel down or unmotivated, clinical depression is characterized by **prolonged** feelings of low mood, changes in appetite or sleep patterns, a "slowed" pace with work or other activities, self-destructive behavior, feelings of guilt or shame, social withdrawal, sadness, frequent crying, and distractibility. The National Institutes of Health study on depression (1997) suggest that almost one in seven individuals who are clinically depressed will commit an act of violence. Most frequently, this will be the act of suicide, although homicide and combined suicide/homicide are occurring with increasing frequency.

Bipolar depression is another mood disorder where individuals not only experience the painful lows of clinical depression, but also experience manic "highs" where there is increased irritability, expansive or elevated mood. These individuals will manifest their symptoms in inflated and grandiose presentation, decreased need for sleep, excessively fast speech, racing thoughts increases in goal directed activity, i.e., work, sex, etc., spending sprees and other impulsive and excessive behavior (DSM-IV, 1994). Left untreated, individuals with this disorder can become psychotic or "out of touch" with reality and experience psychotic symptoms such as delusions, paranoia, and hallucinations; as with any psychotic disorder judgment and the ability to accurately evaluate the consequences of one's actions decreases, increasing the potential for impulsive behavior.

> **Personality Disorders**

Baron (1993) noted that personality has been defined as "consistent human patterns within the individual." These patterns are lifelong, pervasive and central to whom we are and how we think, perceive, and relate. Personality has a tremendous impact on how we function in relationships, in the world and at work. We all have personality patterns that dictate our choices and our behaviors. However, when this enduring pattern of thinking and relating deviates from the norm, and becomes inflexible, impaired, distorted and unhealthy, these traits can become personality disorders and can reduce effectiveness in functioning emotionally, cognitively and in relationships. The *Diagnostic and Statistical Manual of Mental Disorders* (1994), Fourth Edition (DSM-IV) describes the general criteria for a personality disorder as "an enduring pattern of experience and behavior that deviates markedly from the expectations of the individual's culture." The impairment is manifested in at least two of the following four ways: cognition, emotions, interpersonal functioning and impulse control. The pattern is enduring and inflexible, and pervasive across a broad range of situations, and leads to impairment in "social, occupational or other important areas of functioning." Two disorders in particular are associated with potential workplace violence.

❖ **Antisocial Personality Disorder**.

Often described as "sociopaths," these individuals tend to manifest behavior that is irritable, aggressive, and in clear violation of the rights of others. More common in males than in females, individuals with this disorder frequently fail to conform to social norms for behavior, and often have difficulties with the law, including repeated arrests. It is not uncommon for these individuals to have histories of physical altercations at home, at work and in other social venues. Drug and alcohol abuse is common, and these individuals are not adverse to stealing, destroying the property of others, or harassing or physically assaulting those with whom they come into contact. Generally, these individuals will have little remorse about their behavior, and may only appear regretful when there are punishments imposed upon them. They will often justify their behavior, and blame others when things go wrong. Frequently charming and charismatic upon first meeting, these individuals fail to maintain solid relationships. Their job histories are often spotty. They may have a job for several months, then leave or be fired, stay unemployed for a period of time, and then find another job. These individuals have frequent absences from work, and are likely to steal or vandalize company property.

❖ **Borderline Personality Disorder.**
　　Essentially, those with Borderline Personality Disorder will exhibit a pattern of unstable relationships, lack of proper personal boundaries, and poor impulse control. Their behavior is often perceived by others to be erratic, over-emotional, inappropriate and, at times, dramatic. This individual will often experience severe mood shifts, intense anger and even rage, and in more severe cases, suicidal or self-mutilating behavior. Again, substance abuse and addictive behaviors are common in individuals with this disorder. They are preoccupied with themselves and will use others to achieve their goals and desires. There is often uncertainty regarding relationships, identity, career choices, values, and even sexual orientation. They frequently experience chronic feelings of emptiness and isolation, and fear abandonment from others. In the workplace, the borderline individual's behavior can be manifested in erratic and dramatic actions in response to conflict, to perceived slights from others, to being passed over

for promotions or raises, or to disciplinary action or termination. While angry, the borderline personality is likely to act impulsively, inappropriately and most often with retaliatory purpose.

> ## Post Traumatic Stress Disorder (PTSD)

At the conclusion of the Vietnam War, doctors and clinicians noted a significant number of psychiatric casualties in veterans who have served in combat. The symptoms observed by these professionals included anxiety, "flashbacks" to horrifying events, depression, and emotional numbing, to name a few. Similar syndromes had been observed and recorded in relation to previous wars. The term "battle fatigue" was often used to describe the emotional sequel that not infrequently followed wartime military duty. The label used to describe a syndrome of symptoms following a traumatic event, is now called Post Traumatic Stress Disorder (PTSD). Individuals who experience PTSD have been exposed to a traumatic event in which the individual "experienced, witnessed or was confronted with an event or events that involved actual or threatened death or serious injury, or threat to the integrity of self or others, and in which the person's response was intense fear, helplessness or horror" (DSM-IV, 1994). This traumatic event can be not only exposure to combat, but also occurrences like car accidents, industrial trauma, severe physical or emotional abuse, or any other life-threatening situation. Individuals diagnosed with PTSD demonstrate higher rates of depression, suicide and homicide than the general population. This places them at a higher risk for becoming perpetrators of workplace violence.

> ## Substance Abuse/Chemical Dependency

Drugs and alcohol impair an individual's ability to make accurate decisions and judgments, increase agitation and emotionality, and decrease the normal inhibitory process with regard to behavior and social conduct. Additionally, drugs and alcohol can increase paranoia and aggression. Based on published studies, Roizen (1997) summarized the percentage of violent offenders who were drinking at the time of their offense. Alcohol was a factor for violent offenders in 86% of homicides, 37% of assaults, 60% of sexual assaults, and 13% of child abuse. Additionally, 57% of men and 27% of women were using alcohol while committing their respective violent acts. A community-based study found that 42% of violent crimes reported to the police involved alcohol, although 51% of the victims who were interviewed believed that their assailants were drinking at the time of the offense (Pernanen, 1994). Co-occurrence of substance abuse and anti-social and borderline personality disorders is common. Thus, individuals who may exhibit marginal functioning at best may be pushed over the edge when drugs and/or alcohol are involved (Baron, 1993). In many cases of workplace violence, drugs and alcohol, often in combination with a psychotic disorder (see below) appeared to have played a significant part in the perpetrator's behavior.

➢ **Psychosis**

Generally speaking, a person who is psychotic has lost contact with reality. *Psychotic Disorders* include schizophrenia, some depressive disorders, some bipolar depressive disorders, and paranoid and delusional disorders. As mentioned above, depression and bipolar disorder can, in severe cases, result in a loss of contact with reality; however, these disorders primarily involve a mood disorder.

Individuals with schizophrenia often manifest that disorder in a number of ways. Tangential thinking and loose associations, disordered speech, catatonic or disorganized behavior, flat facial expressions, and odd beliefs and thoughts are common in schizophrenia, as are auditory and visual hallucinations, and bizarre delusions (DSM-IV, 1994). For example, schizophrenic individuals may believe that their television is "talking" to them and transmitting secret messages about what they are to do, or whom they are to trust. In paranoid schizophrenia, a persecutory delusion, or delusion that others are "out to get me" is predominant.

Paranoid and Delusional Disorders are another category of psychotic disorders. *Paranoid Disorders* are demonstrated in the individual who is convinced, irrationally, that someone or everyone is out to get him or her, or who operates with a pervasive sense of mistrust and hostility toward others. *Delusional Disorders* of significant concern include the grandiose type, the jealous type, the erotomanic type and the persecutory type. The *grandiose* individual believes that he or she has insights, knowledge or powers that no one else has. The *jealous* type is irrationally convinced that his or her lover or spouse has been unfaithful (Baron, 1993), and refuses to believe otherwise, despite contrary evidence. The *erotomanic* person maintains the fantasy and the delusion that another individual, sometimes a public figure, is in love with him or her. These individuals are often involved in stalking cases. Those of the *persecutory* type often have a long history of resentment toward a person or organization they feel has wronged them in the past. They will magnify the perceived slights or injustices from others, and will attempt to achieve "justice" through legal means (i.e., lawsuits, criminal charges) and illegal means (i.e., vandalism, aggression, violence). All of these individuals have the potential for violence as a means of achieving "justice," vindication, or attention and should be taken very seriously.

CASE STUDY:
Mark had a cache of assault weapons at home. Based on his military training, he considered himself an expert in the use

of weapons. Psychologically, Mark was obviously suffering and impaired socially and occupationally. His behavior was not normal. Had he been evaluated and diagnosed, the organization would have found that Mark suffered from post-traumatic stress disorder (PTSD) as a result of his Vietnam War experiences. Left untreated, his rage did not abate. His alcoholism, a common factor among those who suffer from PTSD, increased his potential for violence.

IV. Limited or Non-Existent Coping Skills

An Inability to Deal with Normal Daily Stress – Each of us deals daily with many stressors. We meet challenges at home, at work, in our relationships, with our health, our kids, and our finances, to name a few. Generally, we are able to work through these issues and eventually develop solutions to resolve them. Most people have adequate coping mechanisms that allow them to address problems successfully. However, those whose emotional and mental instability interferes with normal thought processes may experience life events, which compound to the point that they become overwhelmed, losing the capacity to cope with these issues. Often, in an attempt to cope with these stressors, they choose maladaptive ways to address the difficulties in their lives. These can include drugs and alcohol, social isolation, self-mutilating behavior, aggressive and threatening behavior, and illegal behavior. These maladaptive solutions are a faulty attempt to gain some perceived control over their lives. It is difficult for these individuals to identify solutions to their problems that consist of options other than violence to themselves or to others.

Overreaction to Negative Events - Everyone reacts to negative events that affect their lives. It is certainly normal for any of us to get upset when something unpleasant happens. However, when one's reaction is out of proportion to the event, this constitutes a "red flag" that something more than the incident that touched off the behavior is occurring. Some individuals will overreact to the slightest negative issue, or perceived negative issue, and can turn to violence as a means for releasing their tension.

CASE STUDY:

Mark's emotional reaction to Joan's denial of his request for the day off, coupled with her requirement for him to submit medical documentation for his leave, was out of proportion to the situation. He was simply unable to cope with these normal daily stresses. His overreaction flashed a sign that needed to be addressed. He exhibited behavior that showed impaired coping mechanisms, impulsive behavior, and despair and hopelessness - common signs of PTSD. In Mark's case, his reaction to Joan's denying him the day off was well out of proportion to the news that he was needed to work that day. He lost control – an indication that his coping skills were nearly non-existent.

V. Limited or Non-existent Support Systems

Inaccessibility to adequate social support systems places individuals at further risk for perpetrating an act of workplace violence, particularly in combination with some of the other ingredients for workplace violence, which have already been discussed. The following are some areas of support which, when lacking, can be critical contributors to a violent incident:

➢ **Work Related Systems** – For many of us, most of our waking hours during the week are spent at work. When problems occur in an employee's personal life, this can often spill over into his or her work performance. Many organizations provide programs and training to assist their employees with their personal stressors and corporate communication issues. Other employers decide not to provide employee assistance programs, give training related to working effectively in groups, or maintain security measures. Unfortunately, these decisions result in the lack of a "safety net" through which organizations can intervene when an employee is experiencing coping problems. A series of negative events, mental illness, alcoholism, drug abuse, threatening behavior and/or long-term unresolved conflict can combine to create a potential "time bomb" waiting to be ignited. When a company recognizes signs of distress, intervenes and offers resources to the potentially explosive individual, there is a greater chance that a work-related tragedy can be averted.

CASE STUDY:

In Mark's case, management did not have any idea as to what was going on between Mark and his supervisor, Joan. Supervisors were not trained to safely address the problems of inappropriate behavior displayed by Mark. When his superiors felt that they had exhausted their resources for managing Mark, he was sent a discharge letter. Little did they realize the potential results of that action.

Family & Relatives - The traditional make-up of the American family has changed over the years. We have many more dysfunctional relationships, fewer extended family structures, frequent divorce, greater financial pressures, and looser emotional connections with each other. Parents are often unable to spend as much time as they would like with their children; children frequently spend more time in front of the television than they do interacting with parents and sib-lings. While at one time, extended families often lived within the same communities and geographical areas, now families are typically spread out in many different directions. The impact of these trends has been that more people than ever are trying to deal with their problems without help from family.

Many articles and editorials have been written on the deterioration of the family structure. The erosion of the family structure in the United States has had an impact on violent behavior by reducing the support system, which, in the past, restricted and penalized inappropriate behavior. For instance, when a child misbehaved at school or an adolescent encroached on the rights of another family member, there were consequences imposed by the family and often, the greater social structure. Conversely, when family members were experiencing problems, they could count on a support system to help them through their difficulties, creating viable options for coping. The erosion of the system that had, in the past, provided both limits and support, has likely contributed to an increase in violent behavior.

Some individuals feel they cannot rely on others, even on family members. Others may feel that it is a sign of "weakness" to ask for assistance. As a result, more people are internalizing their problems and subsequently feeling more isolated. Without accessing the support of family, people often feel as though they have fewer resources and options for coping with the stress and tension of their lives.

Friends – The United States is not a "kinder, gentler" nation. Communities and neighborhoods have become increasingly impersonal, disconnected and uncaring. One often hears that many of those who kill co-workers, supervisors and managers were "loners." What this nametag really means is that they had no support system to help them deal with their problems. In some cases, a lack of friendships or close relationships can also signify deeper emotional problems as demonstrated by an inability to develop and sustain meaningful relationships. In either case, friends are a key support system, and another safety net to help prevent violence in the workplace. Talking to friends tends to de-escalate problems, either by providing solutions, or by putting situations in their proper perspective and offering an objective view of problem-solving options.

Chapter 2

CASE STUDY:

Mark had no friends, and his wife was unable to help him. Their marriage was in a desperate situation and needed immediate marital counseling intervention if it was to be saved. Her brother acted as the support net, intervening to stop Mark from carrying out his desperate plan. The good news in this case was that Mark's support system, as loose as it was, saved Joan's life.

Institutions - When an employee is unaware or unwilling to access institutions such as employee assistance programs, mental health agencies, churches, Alcoholics Anonymous, United Way, or other social services designed to assist anyone who is experiencing problems, the potential of the employee's resorting to violent behavior is increased. A factor that has influenced the availability of institutional resources has been the recent budget cuts for social service and welfare programs. Low or no cost resources have become increasingly difficult to find. Additionally, the advent of managed care has significantly limited the scope of mental health services, which would likely benefit troubled employees.

Medical - The lack of medical intervention in dealing with an employee who is potentially violent is a key factor in many of these disastrous events. Sometimes, when behavior becomes concerning, there are serious medical or psychological issues involved. In these cases, unless there is a medical evaluation and treatment of employees who threaten others, exhibit inappropriate behavior, or display many of the warning signs stated earlier in this book, the problem will not go away. Many employers think that they are addressing a problem when they immediately fire an employee who threatens his/her supervisor or acts out aggressively. In reality, the employer has lost an opportunity to avoid a potentially triggering event and to manage an effective transition process that can be mutually beneficial for all parties.

CASE STUDY:

Mark's case is a classic example of what not to do. He was viewed as the "problem." He was discharged without any professional having assessed what was really occurring emotionally for him. If he had been diagnosed and treated earlier, his discharge might not have been necessary. Either his inappropriate behavior would have been resolved, or he would have been discharged "safely." The organization put its employees at risk.

VI. Actual or Perceived Negative and Stressful Events

The triggering event can be an isolated severe altercation or an accumulation of perceived negative events. We often read about an employee who kills his supervisor after a negative evaluation, a firing, or a layoff. Fortunately, most of us deal constructively with negative events. As a witness to this assertion, thousands have been laid off recently and have not killed anyone, and millions deal successfully with negative events each day of their lives. For the most part, incidents of workplace violence are not a reflection on society, organizations or managers, but instead a revelation of the inability of the employee to deal rationally and nonviolently with his or her problem. The triggering event is merely the "last straw." The real cause of workplace violence is much deeper, and may be traced back to the other ingredients described earlier.

Financial - Inability to pay bills, bankruptcy, gambling debts, alimony payments, and IRS problems are contributory triggers for those who would resort to violence, either against themselves or against another people. Disciplinary action, job suspension and termination can cause or aggravate current financial stressors. This threat is often perceived as insurmountable, and for individuals who commit acts of workplace violence, other options simply do not exist.

Chapter 2

Domestic – As alluded to previously, domestic disputes and violence also contribute to the incidence of workplace violence, as more and more of these disputes spill into the workplace. Ex-partners are killing former spouses and lovers at their desks at alarming rates. All too often, co-workers get in the way and are also injured or killed. Homicide is now the leading cause of death for women who are killed in the workplace; in 1996, domestic disputes constituted one-sixth of these cases (National Census of Fatal Occupational Injuries, 1996). Domestic violence is also a major contributing factor to other types of problems that affect employee safety and performance, such as child abuse and neglect, substance abuse, homelessness, and psychological illness.

Negative Workplace Issues - Unresolved conflict, poorly trained managers, forced retirements, layoffs, downsizing, discharges, and other employment issues not handled properly are a few examples of the triggers which have led a violent, enraged employee to become verbally and/or physically abusive.

CASE STUDY:

Mark's discharge was his "last straw." The pressure for Mark was so intense that there was only one solution. He saw no way, other than killing Joan, to resolve his problem. Yet the discharge was the trigger, not the cause, of Mark's rage. Had they been properly trained, his supervisors could have handled his discharge more effectively.

Rejection of a Romantic Obsession Relationship - Some workplace homicides have been triggered by a romantic obsession, which reached the final stages of its progression. Normally these relationships, from the obsessor's view, move from positive fantasy through frustration, when the object of the fantasy does not respond reciprocally, to intense anger. Attempts to control the object of the obsession are made via threats, sabotage of personal property, including pets, and violent behavior. All too often, the culmination of this behavior is a violent incident resulting in serious injury or death to the victim of the stalking or those close to the victim. In many cases, this has included co-workers who "got in the way."

A Combination of the Above - When several of these events occur simultaneously, the employee becomes overwhelmed and will usually focus on the event that started the downward spiral in his life. In many cases, the employee will focus on the employment discharge that he believes led to his financial, drinking and domestic problems. He may then decide to get even with his employer and kill his manager, supervisor, co-workers or anyone else he believes partially or fully responsible for his distress.

VII. Ineffective Organizational Response

Most of the events that have led to the deaths of co-workers or spouses could have been de-escalated early, if organizations had been prepared with effective responses to inappropriate behavior. Early intervention with constructive organizational systems is a key strategy to maintaining a non-violent workplace. Unfortunately, organizations with no preventative approach to dealing with this problem continue to be exposed to danger.

No Policy & Protocols - Organizations that have no written policies to deal with threats of violence, aggressive acts and the presence of weapons at the worksite are not in a position to respond effectively. Policies prohibiting these types of behavior and procedures designed to investigate threats, aggressive behavior and other policy violations are the cornerstone of any effective violence prevention program.

No Organized Approach to Address Concerns - Many managers and supervisors have no organized way of recognizing and addressing a potentially violent situation. They do not know whom to contact, how to de-escalate angry behavior, get a temporary restraining order, refer a troubled employee to an EAP, or safely discharge an employee. Thus, the organization has become part of the problem, rather than part of the solution.

Dysfunction Within Independent Unit - A plant manager in a location remote from other elements of the organization tries to address a threatening employee. The manager has not taken the proper action and has summarily fired the employee, and is now concerned that the employee will return to shoot him and others. The action of termination may have been appropriate. Yet his initial concerns about the employee should have been addressed with others before the discharge. Instead, he fires the employee and loses control of the situation.

Untrained Managers/Supervisors - Managers and supervisors who are not trained to de-escalate a situation, spot potentially violent behavior or interactions, or take pre-planned action, place their organizations at risk. The Occupational Safety and Health Administration has stated that training is the cornerstone to workplace violence prevention (OSHA, 1995).

No Conflict Management Protocols - Escalating disputes can occur in any work situation. Companies that do not have organizational systems in place, such as Dispute Resolution Procedures, Grievance Processes and Threat Assessment Teams to counter employee conflicts and evaluate and respond to potential dangerousness, add to the potential for violence.

CASE STUDY SUMMARY:
Let's review the ingredients in Mark's case. Mark, a Vietnam Veteran, had several weapons in his home and certainly knew how to use the rifle strapped to his side. Mark had been diagnosed with PTSD (Post Traumatic Stress Disorder). His alcoholism added to his problems, and his periodic angry

outbursts at Joan demonstrated that Mark had no coping skills with which to address his problems at work. His angry reaction was far out of proportion to the issues at hand. The triggering event was the organization's poorly handled discharge action. He had no friends or available support system at work and was unable to negotiate his problems, as he was not being treated for his mental illness. Fortunately, his brother-in-law saved Joan's life by becoming a last-ditch support system. His intervention was the only ingredient that was present to abort Mark's deadly plan. All the other ingredients present - mental illness, no coping skills, negative events, and ineffective organizational response - combined to precipitate a violent reaction.

Before addressing the solutions, keep in mind that the following ingredients for workplace violence, when combined, provide for a very volatile condition which will need to be cautiously defused through planned effectiveness:

The High Risk Person + Weapon Access + Severe Stressors + Limited Support System + Ineffective Organizational Response + Triggering Negative Events = Critical Incident

DISCUSSION QUESTIONS:

1. On what side of the issue do you stand concerning the media and violence? Is it too much or does it really matter? Remember, the media is not the cause of violence but may confirm already impaired beliefs of a perpetrator. How about video games? Do you know what video games your children are using?

2. "People kill, guns do not," the advocates of the National Rifle Association state. "What we need is stricter laws to stop crimes, not more gun legislation," they say. What do you think? Discuss as a group this

issue. How were you raised about guns in the house? One thing seems clear, it is people plus guns that kill!

3.   There seems to be a growing prevalence of two destructive emotions in our society today. One is anger and the other is depression. Have you seen these emotions in your organization? In your colleagues? In yourself? Discuss the reasons for this phenomenon and what can be done about it in your organization.

4.   The very day we are composing this question, two famous sports players have died because of substance and alcohol abuse. One was in football and the other in hockey. Drugs and alcohol problems seem to be everywhere. What programs do you have in your organization to help individuals who struggle with substance abuse or chemical dependency? Is your management trained to recognize signs of substance abuse? Our society is a "pill-oriented" population. Discuss ways you can help those who struggle with this issue.

5.   Take a look at the ineffective organizational responses in this chapter. Out of these five areas, rate your organization from highly effective (5 points); effective (4 points); average (3 points); ineffective (2 points) and desperate situation (1 point). Discuss as a group your findings and the reasons for your rating.

Chapter Three
Who are the Perpetrators
of Workplace Violence?

We have all seen the dramatic headlines about workplace violence. A terminated employee returns to the workplace seeking revenge. A long-time employee who was "never any trouble" suddenly begins a shooting rampage at work and then kills himself. A disgruntled businessman opens fire in a high-rise office building, killing eight and wounding six before taking his own life. Who are the individuals who most frequently commit an act of workplace violence? What types of situations place employers at higher risk? What are the potential warning signs that an employee poses a danger to the organization?

The Chronically Disgruntled Complainer (Hostile Individual)

These are the cases we hear about most frequently. Sometimes described as "revenge attacks," these are incidents that involve employment-related issues directed toward co-workers, superiors, and/or the organization as a whole. Often these perpetrators have chronic disciplinary histories, poor interpersonal relationships and a history of impulsive behavior. Reactive and hostile are two words frequently used to describe the personalities of these individuals. Additionally, these are people who tend to act out their aggression against others; they will tend to be verbally abusive and may have a history of violence and substance abuse. These are individuals who are most likely to commit an act of violence as an impulsive expression of anger and resentment, rather than "plotting and planning" an act of aggression over a long period of time.

The Loner (Disdainful Individual)

"Quiet, keeps to himself, does his job and goes home." The disdainful individual may work at an organization for years without anybody "really knowing him." Often described as "loners" and "hermits," these are people who keep a very low profile, often have no friends within the organization, and project an arrogant and removed personality to others. Unlike the hostile individuals, the disdainful type will not behave in an emotionally reactive manner and rarely have a history of violence. Rather, they will appear to others as calm, quiet and introverted. These are the individuals who are most likely to "plot and plan" an act of violence. Layoffs after long-term employment and perceived slights or injustices from others can be typical triggers for violence with this type of perpetrator.

The "Profile"

Baron (1993) describes the "typical" demographic and psychological profile of a perpetrator of workplace violence, based upon a review of over 500 case studies. *The following profile is a generalization; certainly, individuals who do not fit this profile are capable of committing acts of workplace violence.* However, as we look at the circumstances surrounding many of the workplace violence incidents that have occurred over the past ten years, the characteristics of these types of individuals remains quite consistent. The typical perpetrator of workplace violence:

- Is generally male
- Has a history of violence (but not necessarily a criminal record)
- Is a loner
- Owns several guns

- Has requested some type of assistance in the past
- Is an angry person with few outlets for expressing that anger
- Has a history of interpersonal conflict
- Is socially withdrawn and has a history of family and marital problems
- Will, after a while, stop expressing himself verbally and become introverted, where perhaps earlier he consistently verbalized his complaints to management and about management
- Is paranoid
- Engages in self-destructive actions, such as drug and alcohol abuse or risk-taking behavior.

Almost always, the individual who has committed an act of homicidal violence has fit some aspect of this profile at the time of the incident. There are two other types of perpetrators of workplace violence who may fit some of the characteristics described above – perpetrators of domestic violence and romantic obsession. These types of incidents are occurring with increasing frequency and pose a serious threat to workplace security.

Domestic Abuser

As previously mentioned, homicide is currently the leading cause of death for women who are killed at work. A recent Department of Labor study showed that in 17% of these deaths, the alleged assailants were current or former *husbands who came into the workplace to kill or injure their partners.* Often, those in the workplace who "are in the wrong place at the wrong time" are injured or killed also. When women are at work, their partners know where they can be found. This places not only the victims at risk, but also the entire workforce at risk.

Romantic Obsessor (Stalker)

Many of us have heard about stalking cases. Romantic obsessors believe that the object of their attraction, whether it is a co-worker, supervisor, acquaintance or even a celebrity, is in love with them. The particularly dangerous issue here is that the object (who could be your employee) of the stalker may be unaware of the high degree of romantic attraction felt by the stalker. Most often, evidence that the object of the attraction is not interested is not enough to deter the stalker. Behavior generally escalates and may start with letters or other written communication and intensify into harassing phone calls, faxes, attempted personal contact, threats and sometimes, assault.

Warning Signs of Potentially Violent Individuals
Threatening Statements

A common misconception about workplace violence is "if they talk about it they're not going to do it." Threatening statements have *very frequently* preceded violent attacks in the workplace and should be taken quite seriously. Threats can be direct (I am going to blow this place up tomorrow), indirect (something bad is going to happen around here), conditional (if 10% raises are not approved by the board, there'll be hell to pay), and implausible (I have a nuclear warhead in my backpack, so don't make me angry). No matter how implausible threats may seem, all threats should be investigated.

Intimidating Behavior

Intimidating and aggressive behavior is another warning sign that should be taken seriously. Employees who attempt to frighten other employees with verbally or physically aggressive behavior, who threaten retaliation if co-workers attempt to intervene or who engage in controlling and manipulative behavior can pose a significant threat to the workplace.

History of Violence

One of the best predictors of violent behavior is a history of violent behavior. An individual who has a background of criminal violence, domestic violence, gang violence, or childhood abuse is at greater risk of perpetrating future violence. The probability of future violence increases with each criminal act (Baron, 1993). Three issues are particularly important with regard to history of violence. The first is recency, that is, the more recently the individual has engaged in a violent or threatening act, the more likely that individual is to engage in aggressive behavior in the near future. The second issue is frequency, the more frequently the individual has been violent or aggressive, the more likely it is that the person will be violent in the future. The third issue is intensity, the more intense the current inappropriate behavior is compared to the last behavior, the more the level of potential danger increases. In assessing any individual for the probability of future violence, these three issues are crucial indicators of behavioral potential.

Obsession with Weapons

Quite frequently, individuals who have committed serious acts of workplace violence have demonstrated an obsession with weapons, most commonly, firearms. This obsession is often evidenced by extensive collections of guns and gun paraphernalia, and/or the individuals may frequently discuss topics related to guns and firearms, appear preoccupied with "practicing" shooting skill and marksmanship and subscribe to gun and weapons magazines such as *Soldier of Fortune.* Additionally, these are individuals who are often times fascinated with stories of war, combat and police activity. They are most frequently not active military or law enforcement personnel, but may be "hangers on" or "wannabes" to those who are.

Recent Marked Performance Decline

What is often noticed is the employee who historically has had a good-to-excellent performance record in the past but more recently has been struggling to meet the requirements of the job, or has been making mistakes or errors that were not previously an issue. Other signs of impaired and declining performance include missing deadlines, losing or misusing work materials, and poor use of work time.

Personality Changes/Changes in Grooming and Behavior

Emotional outbursts, unpredictable behavior, inappropriate remarks or major changes in mood or demeanor are some of the changes observed in potentially violent individuals. Other issues to be alert for are marked changes in grooming habits: dirty or unkempt clothes, ceasing to wear makeup, not bathing regularly, no longer shaving or doing one's hair when previously it was important to the individual to maintain a well-groomed appearance. These are all signs of significant personality change and a regression in functioning.

Paranoia or Entitlement Mentality

Paranoia refers to a pervasive sense of distrust, a persistent feeling or ideation that an individual or individuals are "out to get" the paranoid person. Paranoid individuals may resort to violence to "right the wrong" or gain retribution for perceived injustices. In the most common type of paranoid disorder, the persecutory type, individuals may harbor a long-standing sense of resentment and anger toward a person or organization that they feel has slighted them in the past. Entitlement refers to the sense that the individual deserves special privileges, exemption from organizational rules and policies and special treatment and consideration. For example, a long-term employee may feel that he or she is not bound to the same attendance requirements as other employees, or is entitled to better benefits or a two-hour lunch because of his or her tenure or position with the company. When they are held to the same standards as other employees, such individuals become angry, resentful and sometimes, vengeful.

Serious Stress in Personal Life

Almost universally, when we examine cases of workplace violence, we find evidence of serious stressors in the individual's personal and/or professional life. Financial stressors, marital problems, parenting dilemmas, psychiatric problems and serious health difficulties are weighty issues which can contribute to an individual feeling depressed, out of control, and frustrated. When stressors such as these are combined with perceived unfair treatment at work and other workplace issues, they can ignite volatile behavior. Some examples which may suggest significant stress for an employee include: crying frequently on the job, asking for salary advances, spending much of the workday on the phone with personal issues, receiving calls from bill collectors at work, recent divorce, legal problems and the loss of a loved one.

Evidence of Possible Substance Abuse

As mentioned earlier, drugs and alcohol impair an individual's ability to make accurate decisions and judgments, increase agitation and emotionality, and decrease the normal inhibitory process with regard to behavior and social conduct. Police officers across the country will tell you about the correlation between crime and alcohol and/or drugs. Having an employee who is actively using these substances and who fits even one of the previously mentioned risk factors significantly increases risk for some type of inappropriate or potentially aggressive act in the workplace. Signs of employee substance abuse include mood swings, erratic behavior, long lunches, frequent absenteeism and tardiness, meeting others in remote areas, financial problems, and secretive behavior.

Continual Blaming of Others and Excuses for Behavior

Most often, individuals who have committed acts of workplace violence have a strong external locus of control. That is, they blame others for most or all of their difficulties in life rather than accept appropriate responsibility for their decisions or behaviors. Warning signs in this area include difficulty accepting responsibility for even the most benign of issues, and the individual who consistently blames those around him or her for problems and difficulties.

Poor On-The-Job Relationships

The way in which an individual relates, communicates and interacts with those around him can be significant indicators of potential trouble. Poor on-the-job relationships are evidenced by belligerent behavior, frequent verbal or physical altercations, withdrawal, and overreaction to criticism or feedback. Co-workers or supervisors might describe the individual as difficult, demanding, manipulative or verbally abusive.

Demanding of Supervisor's Time

If a supervisor spends an inordinate amount of time with a particular employee, engaged in coaching, counseling or disciplinary activity to no avail, this is a warning sign that the employee may need help which is outside of the supervisor's scope of expertise. For example, medical or psychological interventions may be warranted. These are specialized areas in which a supervisor is not prepared or trained to intervene, and the employee should be referred for outside evaluation.

Safety Issues

Apparent disregard for personal safety increases in the number and severity of accidents, and recklessness with company vehicles and property, are all signs of stress. All accidents and safety incidents should be investigated thoroughly, and be considered a potential warning sign of other difficulties.

SUMMARY

The presence of at least several of the characteristics of the potentially violent individual presented in this chapter were evident in almost all documented cases of workplace violence. Awareness of employee's behavior, workplace relationships and stress levels are key factors in early problem identification and intervention.

DISCUSSION QUESTIONS:

1. Discuss the typical perpetrator of workplace violence. In your own words, state at least five key factors you can remember about a potential perpetrator.

2. What can the organization do about domestic abuse? Remember, domestic abuse is not simply a private issue, it is a social issue that strikes companies in the United States daily. What programs do you currently have that can help the victim? Do your employees know about these programs?

3. Recent state and federal laws are very clear about stalking and the statistics demand a sober attention to it. Yet, the tendency is to ignore stalking cases because of a myth that this crime happens only to the rich and famous. Discuss the psychological impact stalking has on the victim. What steps can the organization take to assist a victim?

4. Discuss the comment, "everyone makes threats." Is it true? What is the difference between direct, indirect, conditional, and implausible threats?

Go through the list of 18 warning signs of potentially violent individuals. Do you know anyone like this now? How about in the past? How did they get along at work? Were they happy? How did they respond to authority?

Chapter Four
Workplace Violence and
Organizational Effectiveness

Organizations need to develop a systematic approach to dealing with potentially violent employees in order to protect the work force and maintain a safe workplace. Now that we are aware of the ingredients of workplace violence, the solutions can be constructed to reduce the risks. Although individual risk factors can and will continue to exist, specific preventative processes and systems can and should be put in place by organizations, thus aborting the likelihood of an act of workplace violence.

Organizational Culture
The systems in organizations can either contribute to their chances for violence or reduce their risks. Culture in the organization influences behavior, therefore, it is important to keep a pulse on the culture of your organization and maintain systems that enhance its health, as well as addressing issues of potential violence.

Executive "Buy In" - In any organization, both formal and informal expectations for conduct and performance come from the "top down." In order to promote and enforce any safety policy, including a workplace violence policy, there must be the "buy in" or conviction from the executive levels of the organization that the policies and procedures are timely, important, reflect a high priority and are to be followed by all employees at all levels of the organization. Without the crucial endorsement of the company's leadership, it will be very difficult to have managers and employees take seriously and follow through on safety programs, even when they are represented in formal policies. Employees look to their managers, supervisors and other significant figures for cues, verbal and non-verbal, about appropriate behavior and conduct in their workplace.

Employee Opinion Surveys - Many organizations use either formal or informal opinion surveys to track and address employee issues. Paying close attention to employee concerns is not only good business, but is also a necessary strategy for reducing the risks of violence. Whether a simple focus group technique or formal questionnaires are used, such concerns as how supervisors interact with and treat employees, safety, working conditions, fairness of treatment, job stress, sexual harassment and discrimination issues must be closely monitored and problem spots remedied.

Conflict & Dispute Resolution System - Festering, unresolved conflict increases the risk of potential violence. When employees feel they have been unjustly treated, and are allowed to focus on the issue for months or years because of the inefficiency of an extended dispute resolution process, fuel is added to their fire. This is a circumstance that can lead to a violent incident, particularly if the employee eventually loses the prolonged battle and becomes enraged. At that point, he or she may begin to plan retribution. Swift conflict resolution will reduce the negative focus, allowing each party involved to move toward the future. Prolonged dispute resolution processes keep the emotionally enraged employee focused on the past issues and the present dispute, not allowing them to focus toward the future.

Empowerment of Employees - Employees who have some control over the decisions related to their work are less likely to become chronically frustrated and behave in an inappropriate manner. It is important to ask employees for their thoughts and ideas in determining how to make a decision or solve a problem, which directly affects the way that they work. Making employees active in seeking solutions will reduce the tendency to point fingers at higher-level managers.

Management Sensitivity

In a review of recent cases of workplace violence in 1999, most of the ingredients discussed earlier in this book were present. Employees had signs of mental illness often exhausting their coping skills. Most had no effective support system. In many cases, the organizations were unprepared to defuse these potentially violent situations. If managers had been more aware of the employee's concerns, they would have found that the atmosphere at their locations was boiling over with stress, employee mistreatment, and uncaring management teams. Addressing those issues with a careful, caring violence prevention plan might have made the difference for them between life and death.

Compensation & Reward Systems - Managers' rewards drive their behavior. If they are rewarded based solely on company profits, they will not pay attention to how they treat employees, and financial priorities will outrank interpersonal priorities. Balance in these two areas is important. Organizations must make money to survive and grow, but they must also cultivate trust, motivation and loyalty among employees to maximize profits. It is important to review managerial reward systems to insure they are not only producing business results, but are also motivating proper managerial behavior and ultimately, employee investment in the company.

Managerial Selection Criteria – Most often, managers and supervisors are selected based on their education, experience and/ or technical skills. Interpersonal and communication skills as management selection criteria are typically given less importance. However, employing managers who have difficulty relating to their employees, or who have authoritarian and pedantic management styles, will increase the likelihood of problems within that department and ultimately the organization. Selecting managers and supervisors who have effective human relations skills will reduce the risks of ongoing conflict and aggressive behavior. If managers or supervisors do not have ready skills to cope with employees who present risks, the chances are increased that conflict will be ongoing in the workplace, and may lead to violence.

Performance Feedback Processes - Many organizations are using "360° feedback systems" which allow for employees and peers to express their views anonymously and truthfully about how their managers are functioning on motivational, interpersonal and leadership levels with their employees. Valuable information about potential management problems can be gleaned from this type of process, and can be essential in making the types of changes, which can increase security and safety within an organization. Businesses are wise to invest in this practice, not only for practical reasons, but also as added insurance to provide for the minimization of employee mistreatment.

Management Training - Training is the cornerstone of any good organizational violence prevention plan. Managers and supervisors need to be trained to identify potentially violent employees at the earliest possible levels. Training regarding how to respond to threats, harassment and aggression in the workplace and where to report threats within the workplace are also essential elements in any managerial training program. Additionally, managers and supervisors should be trained on how to safely and effectively respond to emotionally enraged employees, how to safely conduct performance reviews, how and when to terminate employees and what kinds of programs and services are available to assist employees who are experiencing difficulties. In order for a workplace violence prevention program to work effectively, training must occur.

Employee Services and Programs

Professional Employee Assistance Program (EAP) - Every organization should be linked into a professional EAP Service. EAPs assist employees whose work behavior may be adversely affected by personal or psychological problems. The service will be provided to employees free of charge, for a predetermined number of sessions. EAP counseling services are short-term, problem focused interventions, which emphasize brief counseling strategies that are solution focused. This type of counseling emphasizes skills and strengths and encourages practicing new behaviors. Brief counseling also involves setting goals that are achievable in a one to five month period.

The complexities of problems in our society today require an expert support system to identify potentially violent conditions and address them early to avoid a problem. Organizational protocols that link in EAP services are taking a major step toward maintaining a nonviolent workplace. The following criteria are recommended for establishing an EAP that will be a major contributor to an effective violence prevention program:

In-house or Outsourced EAP Services Some larger organizations offer in-house employee assistance programs while other organizations out source EAP services to local EAP providers. Regardless of the type of service, it is important that EAP counselors are well trained in the specialized area of violence risk assessment.

Well-qualified Licensed Professional EAP Counselors –

Choosing qualified clinicians can be difficult for any company. The best organizations have Board Certified or state licensed doctoral level mental health professionals. Individuals at this level of training have Ph.D., M.D., or Psy.D. degrees and have undergone a minimum of 3,000 hours of training in mental health issues. They are the individuals most likely to have experience in some form of violence risk assessment.

Easily Accessible and 24-Hour Service – It is crucial that your EAP offers easy accessibility for employees and 24-hour availability in the case of emergencies. Both the organization and the employees must be able to access professional help during a crisis, and most competent EAP's will offer this service.

Critical Incident Debriefing Expertise – EAPs are the professionals most often called upon to respond following a violent or other critical incident. Often, counseling takes place onsite at the company, and involves specialized individual and group intervention. It is important to make sure that the counselors and therapists working with your EAP have had training and experience in this crucial area so that in the event that these services are needed, they can be provided competently and immediately. Appropriate, caring, quality critical incident debriefing services can save an organization thousand of dollars in post-trauma costs.

Workplace Violence and Sexual Harassment Expertise –
Every EAP should have counselors who have knowledge andexperience in the areas of workplace violence, not only from an individual perspective, but from an organizational perspective as well. Particularly in organizations where there have been repeated incidents of sexual and hostile or aggressive conduct, it is important to assess what organizational factors may be contributing to such an environment. Additionally, it is important to have counselors who have knowledge of the specific risk factors associated with both types of behavior, and who are able to offer

competent intervention steps to both the organization and the individual.

Substance Abuse Professionals – The costs of substance abuse to an organization can be staggering. With the plethora of individuals using drugs and alcohol in our workplaces, competent substance abuse programs are essential. Simply stated, your EAP must offer professional, competent and timely substance abuse assessment and treatment services.

Organizational Savvy - Although many EAP professionals are competent clinicians, they often do not understand the business world. It is vital that an EAP work well not only with employees, but also demonstrate an understanding of how companies function so that they can assist the organization in solving a variety of problems, and intervene not only from an individual perspective, but when appropriate, from an organizational one as well.

Background and Reference Checks During the Hiring Process

Believe it or not, many employers do not conduct background checks on potential new employees. They give many reasons for not doing so. Some companies say that they do not receive meaningful or timely information, and they need people immediately. Others feel that the process would be too costly for their organization to bear. As a consequence, they take unwise risks.

If an employee is hired without a background check and he/she shoots a co-worker or manager, the legal liability for the employer may run into the millions of dollars. If an employer who discharged an employee for threatening or assaulting another worker fails to disclose that fact upon inquiry from a prospective employer, the former employer may be at risk for failing to disclose information about a potentially lethal individual. So, what is the message? Conduct thorough background checks on all new employees before you hire them. Avoid hiring your own problems.

Trained Interviewers - A trained interviewer can detect tendencies in the way applicants handle conflict. Most people will respond honestly to open-ended questions, revealing traits that could set off alarms. Probing life events, job changes and stress points will tip off the prospective employer to any dangers with an applicant, and should be carefully addressed in the hiring process.

Current & Former Employers – Although for legal reasons there has been a recent trend in business to verify only dates of employment and position occupied when providing a job reference, calling former employers, as well as sending them the usual employment verification form regarding questionable cases, can pay dividends. Call former supervisors as well as human resource departments. Inquire as to how the employee has handled difficult situations and whether the supervisor would hire the individual again if given the opportunity. Over-the-phone conversations can be helpful, particularly if you voice your concerns regarding violence and remind employers that they may be legally obligated to reveal any information which involves potentially violent behavior.

Current & Former Residence - Checking former residences may reveal gaps in living conditions. For instance, you may discover that the applicant's former place of residence was the state prison, a fact not disclosed by the applicant.

Credit Record - Poor credit that is job-related could disclose financial problems - a valuable piece of information regarding the applicant's current stresses.

Department of Motor Vehicles - **Driver's license information** could reveal drug or alcohol problems, which should be addressed before hiring an employee. DUI's should be of concern to all employers.

Criminal Records - Checking criminal records is a must. Employers cannot afford to hire an individual who has been convicted of a violent crime.

Military Records - Military records are difficult to obtain. However, if an applicant produces a DD214, revealing an administrative or a dishonorable discharge, it is important to follow up on this information and inquire as to the specific details behind the reason for discharge. This information could point to potential risk.

Medical Examination - Conducting pre-employment medical exams is a critical part of the screening process. If there is any indication that a potential employee has demonstrated inappropriate behavior, or has poor coping skills, the doctor should probe more deeply into the medical history of the applicant. If there is medical evidence of a psychiatric problem, it should be uncovered and addressed in the medical report.

Be sure to check with your legal counsel concerning state laws regarding privacy and hiring. Once approved by your legal department, an organization's employment of the tools described above is sound business practice. The reduction of risk of negative events, one of the ingredients of workplace violence, is an added benefit. Therefore, reducing one ingredient will reduce the overall risk of a violent incident.

DISCUSSION QUESTIONS:

Organizational Effectiveness

1. Discuss what processes your organization has in place to reduce potential violence from occurring. Does your organization conduct background checks on new employees? If not, why?

2. If background checks are not done on new employees, and a new employee commits a violent act, what liability does your company have if this employee was fired for violent behavior while working for a previous employer?

3. Why is it important to know whether an ongoing conflict exists between employees and supervisors in various part of your organization. What should be done about it?

Discuss how an Employee Assistance Program fits into your organization protocols for identifying, reporting and addressing potential violent employees.

Chapter Five
Policies & Procedures
Addressing Threats

In order to maintain a nonviolent workplace, it is critical to establish policies and procedures to address threats. When the airports and airlines were faced with hijackings and bomb threats, they instituted a **zero tolerance policy** at every airport. Today, it is well known that it is not acceptable to even make a joke about a bomb or hijacking a plane. If this does occur, one of three things will happen. The individual will be questioned and sent to jail, sent home or sent to a hospital for evaluation. One thing is for certain: that person will not be allowed to board that aircraft. The zero tolerance policy at airports changed behavior over the years and is a model for behavior modification and workplace violence prevention in the workplace. Zero tolerance policies for the workplace are essential to maintaining a safe work environment. Unfortunately, sometimes policies alone are not enough to deter individuals from aggressive, threatening and at times, violent behavior. When such behaviors do occur, effective protocols and procedures for evaluating such situations and intervening appropriately can make a substantial difference in the outcome. Sometimes, this intervention can be the difference between life and death. In this chapter, we will address the importance of developing, communicating and implementing policies against workplace violence and aggression. We will also discuss the key elements of effective procedures to respond to and investigate threats and aggressive behaviors when they do occur.

Workplace Violence Policies

Every organization must adopt a zero tolerance policy to effectively address threats and violence in the workplace. Unfortunately, we do not live in an age where prevailing social norms and expectations for behavior dictate decency and respect. Rules and limits pertaining to acceptable work behavior must be outlined in policy statements. Policy statements are important for at least two reasons. First, good policies provide clear guidelines for expected behavior, definitions of unacceptable behavior, and outline the penalties for violating the policy. Thus, when the policy is communicated to the employee during new-hire orientation and some other venue, the employee has the standards of conduct clearly spelled out for him or her, ideally before they begin to work for the company. For example, when an employee is hired, the employee should be advised that it is the policy of the organization for each employee to respect others and that threats and aggressive acts are a dischargeable offense. Second, when policies have been communicated, applied and enforced appropriately, they provide the structure for the company to take any corrective action necessary when the policy has been violated.

A "Zero Tolerance" Policy

A zero tolerance policy is a policy that prohibits any type of behavior that could be considered aggressive, threatening or violent by anyone in the organization. This includes behavior such as threats, intimidation, and assaults, even comments that were intended as "jokes" but construed to be threatening by other individuals. A zero tolerance policy would state that any employee found guilty of these acts would be subject to disciplinary action, up to and including termination. The policy of zero tolerance must be clear and widely circulated to all employees. It must be articulated in employee orientation and through supervision at all levels of the organization so there is no question as to the consequences of threatening behavior.

Policy Administration and Enforcement

The most important factor in administering any workplace policy, including a workplace violence policy, is support and endorsement from the executive levels of the company. The policy must be regarded by the leaders within the company as highest priority, and as applicable to everyone within the organization. Further, supervisors and managers should be trained to administer the zero tolerance policy consistently and with effectiveness. They should be proficient in recognizing the behavioral indicators of an employee who may be having problems or is potentially dangerous, and understand the importance of reporting these behaviors to a pre-designated person within the organization, such as a Human Resources representative or someone from the medical department. This training should be integrated into the organization's periodic training and not a one-shot session. It is very important that managers and supervisors receive "refresher" training to keep both their awareness of the issue and their skills in dealing with potentially violent employees current.

Zero tolerance policies <u>must</u> be applied to all employees throughout the organization in a consistent manner to be effective. In other words, the standards of conduct that apply in the mailroom also apply in the boardroom. The CEO of a company must follow the same policies, as does a manager, receptionist or janitorial employee. When employees observe that key policies are applied and enforced across the organization, both vertically and horizontally, they receive the clear message that the policy is important and must be adhered to. In the case of workplace violence, the message must be clear that appropriate action will be taken against inappropriate behavior, especially those involving threats. Conversely, policies that are administered irregularly lead to disparate treatment and confusing messaging to employees and supervisors.

Policies must not only describe the types of behavior prohibited by the policy (i.e., threats, assault, sexually harassing behaviors) but they must also describe what employees and supervisors are mandated to do once they suspect a policy violation. For instance, a policy should outline specifically to whom reports of threats, intimidating behaviors and other prohibited behaviors should be reported. The policy should describe the procedures that will occur following the report of the threat. These include how the threat will be investigated, a statement about confidentiality (that confidentiality cannot be assured to either the reporting party or the alleged perpetrator), how the results of the investigation will be communicated to both the alleged perpetrator and the reporting party, the fact that retaliation against the reporting party is prohibited and a dischargeable offense, regardless of the outcome of the investigation, and any potential outcomes if the investigation reveals that policy has been violated (i.e., written and verbal warnings, fitness-for-duty exam, termination).

Finally, the policy must be communicated not only upon hire, but also periodically for all employees (we recommend a policy review every six months) in the form of training, a newsletter, or other effective means.

SAMPLE WORKPLACE VIOLENCE POLICY

AUTHORITY: This policy is established by the
_____. APPLICABILITY: The policy applies to all_____ employees, and to all individuals who, while not _____ employees, perform work at _____for its benefit. SUMMARY: This policy provides guidelines for responding to violence or threats of violence in the workplace. POLICY: _____ strives to provide employees a safe environment in which to work; therefore, _____ will not tolerate violence or threats of violence in the workplace. All

Chapter 5

weapons, as defined by the Penal Code, are banned from _____ premises. Employees who violate this policy will be subject to disciplinary action up to and including termination. Employees who intentionally bring false charges will also be subject to disciplinary action up to and including termination. Non-employee violations of this policy will be handled in accordance with applicable laws. Supervisors and managers shall employ techniques and skills to defuse threats or violent acts by persons under their supervision. They are expected to understand the factors involved in workplace violence and the warning signs of violent behavior. Supervisors and managers are expected to report threats and violent behavior according to the procedures described below and to take any other appropriate actions as indicated. Supervisors and managers are expected to follow the steps outlined below in responding to staff needs should an act of violence occur in the workplace. All employees shall receive training in skills and techniques and the procedures related to the prevention of workplace violence.

DEFINITIONS: A.   Acts of violence include any physical action, whether intentional or reckless, that harms or threatens the safety of another individual in the workplace.
B.   A threat of violence includes any behavior that by its very nature could be interpreted by a reasonable person as intent to cause physical harm to another individual.
C.   Workplace includes _____.

PROCEDURES:
A.General Roles and Responsibilities
  1.In general:
    a.Any person experiencing or observing imminent vio lence should call emergency services at _____.
    b.Any employee who believes a crime has been commit ted against him/her has the right to report that to the proper law enforcement agency.

c.If one of the parties is a non-employee, notify police or security immediately.

2.Employee:

a.Each employee should report any acts or threats of vio lence to his/her immediate supervisor, _____, _____, or _____. Such reports will be promptly and thoroughly investigated.

b.Each employee should notify his/her supervisor of any restraining orders against individuals that include the workplace.

3.Immediate Supervisor:

a.Must respond to issues related to workplace safety.

b Must contact the appropriate specialist, including _____, _____, or _____ in the event of a potential or actual incident.

B.Threats of Violence:

1The incident must be reported to the appropriate indi viduals.

2.If the event is a criminal act, the recipient of a threat or violent act must report it to the_____ police depart ment.

3.Upon receiving report of a threat or violent act, the recipient's supervisor must immediately orally report the event to _____. Prior to doing so, the supervisor may con sult with other persons such as _____, in order to have a better understanding of the event reported. The super visor will follow instructions from the___, following the oral report. If threats are made about a third party and if that party is unaware that he/she is the object of a threat, the supervisor must at this time inform that party orally.

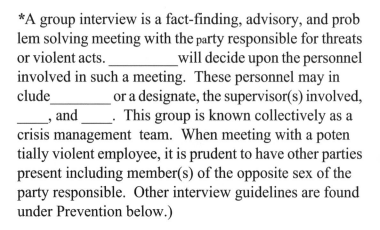

*A group interview is a fact-finding, advisory, and prob lem solving meeting with the party responsible for threats or violent acts. _____will decide upon the personnel involved in such a meeting. These personnel may in clude_____ or a designate, the supervisor(s) involved, ____, and ____. This group is known collectively as a crisis management team. When meeting with a poten tially violent employee, it is prudent to have other parties present including member(s) of the opposite sex of the party responsible. Other interview guidelines are found under Prevention below.)

4.Within two workdays after the event, the recipient of threats or a violent act must complete a Security Incident Report.This Report will be handled pursuant to (refer ence policy here).

5.One of the following responses may follow a report of threats or a violent act:

      a) Counseling or special supervision by the su pervisor
      b) Group interview*
      c)EAP or other treatment referral
      d)Written warning or reprimand
      e)Recommendation for transfer, suspension, de motion or termination
      f)Other action such as change in duty or leave sta tus

6.If a violent employee has been terminated or is on sus-pension or extended leave, and if there is reason to believe he/she may return to the worksite while off duty and commit a violent act, the supervisor of the threatening employee should request immediate changes in office, stairwell or building locks and access codes.

C. Employee Management Procedures:

    1.During the hiring process for all employees, the Employment/Background Reference Checklist should include questioning of previous employers as to whether the candidate has exhibited threatening or violent behavior while employed with them.

    2.Supervisors and managers should make clear with all persons they supervise that threatening or violent behavior is unprofessional and is not tolerated or condoned. The expression of clear expectations in this area can be helpful in discouraging such behavior.

    3.If in the course of supervising an employee a supervisor becomes aware of the warning signs of violence, of mental aberration which could lead to violent acts, or of erratic or intimidating behavior, he/she must document the situation in factual, specific terms, consult up the chain of command, and decide on a course of action from the responses listed above.

    4.In addition, certain other supervision practices can help defuse potentially violent situations. Some of these are:

        a)The supervisor should be alert to changes in attitude and behavior on the part of employees and not be timid about asking if there is a problem.

        b)The supervisor should be sensitive to the potential impact of stress or loss on an employee, understanding that employees can place high value on intangible job perquisites such as privileges, titles, etc., as well as on tangible benefits such as pay raises, parking rights, etc. The supervisor should learn what aspects of employment most motivate or distress those they supervise. Invol untary transfers, loss of pay or benefits, and re ductions of responsibility are personnel actions, which must be approached with care and sensi tivity. (See Preparation, below, for further infor mation.)

c)Employees should always be treated with respect and dignity.

d)Negative personnel actions should be consis tently applied to all employees.

e)Another person should be present in interviews when extremely bad news must be delivered to an employee.

f)The supervisor should be honest and stick to business reasons for taking corrective or other negative personnel actions.

g) The supervisor should avoid use of authoritar ian, intimidating or threatening words or gestures.

h) In cases when an employee must leave the worksite, the supervisor should arrange for a time, after duty hours, for him/her to collect personal property to avoid the employee's embarrassment. A checklist of property to be accounted for and an exit interview with the _____ should be pre pared in advance.

i)Arrange for assistance when an employee leaves, if circumstances warrant.

j) The supervisor should plan for increased con tact with distressed employees unless such con tact would clearly exacerbate the situation.

5.In addition to the Security Incident Report and other Security Procedures noted above, the following Employee Management Procedures should be followed after an in cident of threats or violence.

a)A Crisis Management Team may be formed to investigate the incident in detail and to assess the violence potential of the party responsible. This group shall report to _____ within one week with recommendations as to the proper course of ac tion.

b)The Crisis Management Team, with the approval of _____, may meet with the employee respon sible to discuss the incident and to convey the course of action to the employee.

Procedures

Unfortunately, sometimes policies alone are not enough to deter violent and threatening behaviors. It is important to have procedures in place to deal with policy violations before the need for such procedures actually occurs. It is very difficult to establish effective procedures during a crisis such as a threat of violence; so knowing how to handle these situations ahead of time can help in responding safely and effectively.

♦ *Investigative Procedures*

Chapter 5

All reports of threats, threatening actions, unusual or bizarre behavior, physical assault or any other policy violation must be investigated immediately and professionally. Unlike other types of complaints and policy violations in the workplace, investigating a potentially violent employee can make the difference between life and death. The results of the investigation are very important; they will determine the next step in intervening with the employee and any others who were threatened or harassed. Many companies place the alleged perpetrator on an administrative leave **with pay** until the investigation is complete. There are two reasons for this. First, if the employee does present a threat, that individual should not continue to be in the work environment where she or he may become more agitated during the course of the investigation. An agitated employee at the worksite poses a safety risk. The second reason is that by providing pay during the investigation, the organization is not potentially adding to this person's current stressors. The goals are to keep the individual as stabilized as possible during the investigation and to keep the site safe. It may be appropriate to hire security and even surveillance during this period of time to increase the level of safety for the organization.

There are several issues to address in establishing the organization's procedures for investigating potentially violent employees. The first issue is to determine who will do the investigation. Some companies have their Human Resources and/ or Legal Departments conduct the investigation; others prefer to have outside experts come in to investigate the complaint. There are pros and cons to each approach, and appropriate legal counsel as well as psychological professionals with workplace violence expertise should be consulted in making this decision, and in determining the specifics of how to conduct an investigation of this nature safely and legally. The second issue is to determine how investigations will be conducted. Most investigations involve first interviewing the witnesses to the threat or event, and then interviewing the alleged perpetrator. Based on the information gathered during these interviews, a decision regarding the outcome of the investigation is made. Finally, as a part of outlining the company's investigative procedures, the ways in which the results of the investigation will be communicated to the parties involved is described, as are the possible outcomes and consequences of an investigation in which policy violation was found to have taken place. Every step of the investigation should be documented in writing. All procedures for investigations should be in writing, and documentation of the investigation should follow these written procedures.

♦ Intervention Procedures

It may be determined that the employee did commit a policy violation, but the violation does not warrant termination. The organization should have a menu of options for either disciplining the employee or having the employee evaluated medically or psychologically. Disciplinary actions can include verbal or written warnings, probation periods, increased supervision, demotion, and suspension. In cases where the individual was found to have violated the policy, but there is concern as to his or her psychological or medical well-being (or is he or she exhibiting some of the indicators of higher risk discussed earlier) then a fitness-for-duty exam may be appropriate (see Chapter 8). In most cases, when an employer requires a fitness-for-duty exam, it is recommended that the employee be placed or continue on a paid leave of absence until the results of the exam are determined and communicated back to the employer. As mentioned, in some cases it will be appropriate to maintain added security during this time, as a precaution.

♦ Termination Procedures

In some instances, the results of the investigation reveal that the employee has committed a dischargeable offense. The company feels that it has no option but to terminate the employee.

Chapter 5

The reality is that layoffs and terminations have been the triggers for violent reactions from employees and former employees in previous incidents. Just as policies and procedures are necessary for effectively evaluating and responding to threats in the workplace, it is very important to have procedures in place for terminating potentially dangerous employees. Managers and Human Resource professionals must be familiar with recommended guidelines for conducting terminations. Baron (1993) recommends that the following guidelines be considered when terminating an employee:

- Treat all employees with respect and dignity.
- All disciplinary actions should be applied consistently to all employees.
- Adverse action should be avoided whenever possible if the employee is pregnant, undergoing divorce, or dealing with illness or a recent loss.
- Have another person present when a supervisor or Human Resource person delivers the news of the termination.
- Don't make small talk – stick to the business reasons for the dismissal.
- Terminate at the beginning of the week, at the beginning of the shift (if the employee is considered dangerous, termination should occur at the end of the shift to minimize other employee exposure).
- Don't expect the employee to act rationally.
- Consider the need to have security personnel present. Allow the employee to come back after hours to clean out his/her workstation. Do not allow the employee to go back to their work area unescorted.
- Have all forms and written materials regarding benefits, severance, profit sharing, etc., prepared in advance. Also have the final paycheck ready, and a checklist of property to be returned.
- Rehearse what you are going to say. Be professional at all

times.

- <u>Strongly</u> consider severance and outplacement services for the individual. Termination is stressful. We want to mitigate this impact as much as possible and begin to focus the individual on the future, thereby reducing risk to the organization.
- Be sure to retrieve pass cards and keys, change security codes and computer passwords that were used by the discharged employee.
- Depending on the level of threat, consider having security onsite for a period of time following the termination.

♦ **Downsizing**

The preceding recommendations should also be considered following a downsizing, particularly when management is aware of downsizing a volatile or previously threatening employee. Layoffs, for a variety of reasons, create a lot of stress and anxiety. In addition to considering the factors stated above, it is also important to consider several other factors when planning to downsize. The first is maintaining honesty in information and communication from management. Employees must believe that they are being related to honestly and with integrity and respect. Discuss the reasons for reduction with employees, allow time for questions, and be available in the future to answer questions as they come up. Also, know in advance what services and severance will be offered to employees as they are transitioned out of the company, and communicate these clearly, so that employees will know what to plan for. Many employers are now offering outplacement services through their human resource departments or through outside firms. Finding a good outplacement firm is in the interest of both the organization and the employee – it portrays the employer as caring and concerned, both to the downsized employee and to those who remain in the organization. It also assists terminated employees in organizing their resources and focusing toward the future, rather than staying entrenched in the past, perhaps rooted in anger or resentment toward the former employer. Individuals may be able to obtain new employment more quickly, thereby reducing significant life stress (a potential risk factor), and possibly averting a violent reaction.

DISCUSSION QUESTIONS:

1. Why is it important to have a zero tolerance policy regarding threats and violent behavior? How will a zero tolerance policy help reduce violence?

2. Discuss some specific cases where zero tolerance would apply and what action would be appropriate for organizations to take in such situations.

3. Discuss what policies and procedures your organization has in place to address workplace violence. Are supervisors and employees adequately trained regarding those policies and procedures?

4. What would you do if another employee at work threatened you? Discuss your feelings and concerns.

Chapter Six
Critical Incident Plans & Protocols

In the event of a critical incident, an organization will be viewed by its employees as either a "victim" or a "villain." The differences of perception are largely due to the plans, protocols, and processes for the prevention of violence that the organization has developed and implemented prior to the incident.

It is crucial that each individual organization evaluate where it is likely to be most vulnerable with regard to a violent incident or attack, and develop plans and procedures to address that risk. Violence in the workplace typically takes place in one of three scenarios. First, when an outside person comes into the organization with the intent to commit a crime (Type I); second, when an angry customer, patient or client comes into the workplace and is violent (Type II); third, when an employee is angry with management and returns to "settle a score" or seek revenge (Type III). An organization should consider, based upon past history for the organization and these three Cal/OSHA categories of workplace violence, whether they are most susceptible to Type I, Type II or Type III violence, or some combination thereof, and develop plans and protocols to address potentially violent situations. Plans and protocols should address how the organization, and individuals within the organization, should respond and intervene in a potentially violent situation. Additionally, every organization should have a Trauma Plan as a part of their workplace violence prevention program. The following are aspects of each of these types of plans, which are

85

key elements of this type of program.

Establish Critical Incident Pre-Crisis Plans.

Pre-crisis plans are designed to establish protocols for assessing threats and the potential for violence in the workplace and to minimize the possibility that a threatening situation will escalate into violence or a crisis. Pre-incident plans establish action lists and procedures, roles that various individuals will be assigned in the event that threat assessment or crisis procedures need to be implemented, and the chains of both command and communication in the event that a critical incident does occur.

The elements of the plans focus on the following:

1. Early Intervention Regarding Inappropriate Behavior – Many times, there is a tendency by management and even Human Resource professionals to avoid facing a problem employee and to tolerate inappropriate behavior based on the fear that confronting the employee will escalate, rather than contain, the situation. While for some this is the reasoning or justification for not addressing the problem, the opposite is actually true. Failure to intervene early adds fuel to the fire. The first signs of inappropriate behavior must be addressed and documented. In fact, one of the single most important strategies in preventing incidents of workplace violence is recognizing the early warning signs of problems with employees, and taking steps to address the issues or difficulties at hand. In other words, intervening early, before the behavior escalates, is a strategy that will minimize a need to deal with a problem that has gotten out of hand.

The following is a brief review of warning signs of potentially violent individuals:

> ➢ Threatening Statements

➤ Severe Depression
➤ Psychosis
➤ Paranoia
➤ Substance Abuse
➤ Intimidating Behavior
➤ History of Violence
➤ Obsession with Weapons
➤ Recent Marked Performance Decline
➤ Personality Changes/Changes in Grooming and Behavior
➤ Paranoia or Entitlement Mentality
➤ Serious Stress in Personal Life
➤ Continual Blaming of Others and Excuses for Behavior
➤ Poor On-The-Job Relationships
➤ Demanding of Supervisor's Time
➤ Safety Issues

2. Notification Protocols Regarding Immediate Threat Situations and Behavior That Need Attention and Resolution – The process by which threats, threatening or concerning behavior and aggressive behavior are reported is crucial to the success of any organizational violence prevention program. Supervisors and employees must have a clear understanding that they are mandated to report threatening behavior and policy violations. Equally important is knowing to whom to report. Typically, a human resource representative is designated as the party to whom reports by managers and employees should be made. Some organizations instruct employees to report threats to their direct supervisors. This approach is appropriate, with two caveats. First, employees should not be instructed to report to managers unless the managers have been trained in how to handle the report. Second, an alternative reporting party must be identified to employees, in the case that the manager is the individual who has made the threat, or for some other reason the employee does not feel it

would be efficacious to report the threat to the manager. One model for establishing reporting procedures is exemplified in many standard sexual harassment policies. In the early to mid 1980's, organizations were required to set up protocols to deal with sexual harassment. Today these procedures continue to change but are generally far more effective than several years ago. Awareness training has helped tremendously. The same approach needs to be used in addressing threats and violence.

3. Establishment of Critical Incident Assessment Team A key factor in an organization's success in maintaining a non-violent workplace is the establishment of a team of key employees to manage potentially violent situations before they become 911 calls. Maintaining a non-violent workplace will depend on the establishment of plans and protocols involving a well-trained group. The role of the group is to deal with those difficult and more complex situations regarding employees whose behavior is causing problems and the supervisor is not able to cope with or deescalate the situation. The model of the team, the selection of the key players, the training they receive and the effectiveness of that team will go a long way in preventing incidents from happening in the workplace. These teams are typically referred to as Critical Incident Assessment Teams (CIAT), Threat Assessment Teams (TAT) or Crisis Management Teams (CMT). These terms refer to essentially the same function.

Critical Incident Assessment Team (CIAT)

The purpose of the CIAT is to collect information regarding an employee whose behavior is of concern to management and determine if the employee is potentially violent. If it is determined that the employee is potentially violent, the team develops an action plan to address the situation so as to prevent a violent act from occurring.

The team should have the following representations from the organization:.

Human Resources Manager
Employee Assistance Program (EAP)
Medical
Employee Relations/Legal
Safety/Injury Compensation
Security
Line Management
Professional Threat Assessment Specialists

Depending upon the size of the organization, the representation will consist of internal resources and external resources. Most organizations will normally have designated EAP, Medical, Legal and Professional, and Threat Assessment Specialists as external sources, while the remaining positions will be made up of internal employees from various positions in the organization.

Train the Team on Conducting Organizational Threat Assessments

Once the Critical Incident Assessment Team is established, the members must be trained in conducting organizational threat assessments and how to take effective actions. Threat assessment specialists should present the training. A typical comprehensive threat assessment training will consist of a full three days of course work. Critical Incident Assessment Team Training should consist of:

- The factors which can cause violence to occur
- The warning signs of potentially violent individuals
- The unique role that each member of the team plays
- The organization and the procedures that are in place for dealing with potentially violent situations
- The tools available to effectively reduce the risk of a

violent act occurring and how to use those tools effectively

- ◆ Identification of all resource options that are available to assist in managing potentially critical situations
- ◆ How to continue monitoring situations over a period of time
- ◆ The legal issues involved in threat assessment and intervention
- ◆ Working mock cases to upgrade skills in organizational effectiveness and intervention. Casebooks for groups to utilize are especially helpful when there are no current real-life situations to discuss.
- ◆ The importance of meeting regularly for follow-up training and meetings to keep skills fresh and the team cohesive.

It is important to underscore that the team members should meet regularly in order to remain in operational readiness. They should receive refresher training at least annually in order to remain effective. As members change, the new members must be effectively integrated into the team, and trained in accordance with their peers.

A Success Story

The following is a true story of how effectively a Critical Incident Assessment Team can work to reduce the likelihood of a violent incident. This account is provided with permission to Jim Merrill:

The Human Resource office for the United States Postal Service received a call early one morning from the Postmaster in Antioch, California. The Postmaster stated that she had just received a letter from a former employee which she felt was threatening in its tone and content. She conveyed her concern to the Human Resources Manager and asked for assistance in addressing the matter in an efficient and safe manner.

At the request of the Human Resources Manager, the Postmaster faxed the letter to him for review. The letter from the former employee complained that the organization was harassing him by sending him a letter demanding payment of $1500, which he allegedly owed to the organization before he resigned. He went on to accuse the Postmaster of stealing and further stated that he was surprised that she was "still around" and wondered why she had not been targeted yet by anyone because "she deserved it."

The Human Resources Manager initiated an investigation surrounding the reported threat and the former employee and found that:

- He had been a volatile employee and that he currently had an attorney pursuing the accounting issue regarding the $1500 demand.

- He had "blown off steam" each time he had previously received a letter from the Postal Service, but never escalated his complaint to the point of making threatening comments.

A few days later, the Postmaster received an e-mail from the former employee and forwarded it to the Human Resources Manager. In his e-mail, he asked for help. He indicated that he had been having nightmares and that during these dreams he was walking into the Post Office to kill the Postmaster. He said he had a gun and was seeking treatment by the Veterans Administration in Palo Alto.

Upon receipt of the e-mail, the Human Resources Manager convened the Critical Incident Assessment Team, which consisted of a medical doctor, the Postal Inspector, an EAP Representative, an Employee Relations Representative, and representation from the U.S. Post Office's Legal Counsel. The team reviewed the

Chapter 6

information and made the decision to increase the security in the Antioch Post Office and to transfer the Antioch Postmaster to the District office until the situation had stabilized. One member of the team, the medical doctor, contacted the former employee's current physician at the Veteran's Administration to inform him of the situation and to try to obtain any relevant information about the level of risk that the former employee posed to the organization, while the legal representative of the team worked to obtain a restraining order against the former employee.

The employees in the Antioch Post Office were then briefed on the situation and the steps the organization had taken to insure their safety. When the team re-convened to share information with each other, the team doctor reported that the Veteran's Administration doctor indicated that he was in fact currently treating the former employee and that the former employee was suffering from Post Traumatic Stress Disorder. The physician indicated, however, that in his medical opinion the former employee was not dangerous and he was instead "venting" his anger. The legal representative reported that the restraining order was delivered to the former employee in a non-threatening manner and that the former employee's attorney stated that his client would not violate the order. The organization decided to dismiss the $1500 demand and so notified the former employee's attorney. The Veteran's Administration was advised to alert the company if the former employee subsequently became a safety concern.

After a week of monitoring the situation, the Crisis Management Team decided:

- Return the Postmaster to her office
- Debrief employees
- Return security to normal
- Keep the restraining order in effect indefinitely

- Continue to monitor the case for a several more weeks

After several weeks with no activity, the case was closed.

4. Intervention and Action Plan – Each organization, whether or not it has a Critical Incident Assessment Team, should have a plan to work with potentially violent employees. James S. Cawood, author of "On the Edge: Assessing the Violent Employee" in Security Management, 1991, recommends taking the following actions:

> *Step 1* – Develop a written plan for handling threats. It should specify that reports be made to Human Resources, not a supervisor or manager.

> *Step 2* – Make an immediate investigation by interviewing the person who reports the threat as well as any other witnesses to the incident. Gather as much information as possible about the threat and the person making it. Document this information in detail.

> *Step 3* – Contact a specialist in assessing potentially violent employees to review the information and decide if further action is necessary.

> *Step 4* – If an additional investigation is warranted, form a crisis management team (or contact your existing team).

> *Step 5* – Together with the specialist, develop a plan with this team. This can

include a background investigation of the employee. Emphasis should be directed to locating information indicative of how the employee responds to stress and should consider the indicators of higher risk for violence summarized earlier. Past military service or interest in weapons should be included. The investigation should be handled discreetly to shield the company from later claims of libel, slander, or invasion of privacy.

Step 6 – The specialist should interview the person who reported the threat and any others who can verify or provide additional information on the employee's state of mind. This must be done discreetly so as not to alert the suspected employee.

Step 7 – The employee should be interviewed directly by the specialist. Provide security if it is believed that the employee will become enraged. Security personnel should be experienced and trained to handle the situation. Calm, low-key security individuals who do not project a threatening or officious manner are recommended. Their behavior should not precipitate an incident of violence.

Step 8 – Give the employee the rest of the day off. Give instructions that he/she is not to return to work until approval is received from a designated member of the Crisis Management Team. (As mentioned, we also recommend paying the employee during the period that he/she is off from work. We also recommend that before being sent home, the employee be advised that he/she is not to contact anyone from the organization with the exception of the designated member of the Crisis Management Team, and that violation of this directive will result in termination.)

Step 9 – The Crisis Management Team should meet to review and analyze the information collected. If it is determined that the individual is not a threat to self or others, a decision needs to be made concerning a referral for counseling. For example, should the referral be on a voluntary basis or as a condition of employment? Should the employee be dismissed because of violation of policy?

Step 10 – If the specialist decides that the employee is an immediate danger to self or others, decisions need to be made. Should mental health, EAP or law enforcement be notified? How will the employee's separation from the company be handled? Is the company's position defensible? Should the company seek a restraining order? How should security be involved? How long should security be enforced?

5. Referral to Appropriate Service Providers – If it is determined that an employee is to be referred for counseling, or in some cases, a Fitness-for-duty exam, it is important to have

prescreened providers well before you actually need to use them. For counseling purposes, Employee Assistance Programs (EAP) typically offer a range of psychotherapy and counseling services. Your EAP should offer immediate assistance and appointments in the case of an emergency, chemical dependency services, doctoral-level licensed mental health providers, and most importantly, should offer professionals who have experience interfacing with individuals and organizations. Counseling, and the details of an employee's personal life, should always be a confidential experience. In the case of mandatory EAP referrals, however, the employee should understand that the employer would request information pertaining to whether or not they are attending sessions and whether or not they are following the prescribed treatment plan. A competent EAP or counseling professional with organizational experience will know the appropriate guidelines and protocols for releasing this type of information. Feedback to the organization about how and when the individual is addressing problems related to work performance can be crucial in determining whether or not to retain the employee.

6. Trauma Response Team – While the above procedures and resources are designed to prevent a violent incident from occurring, it is also important for the organization to have a trauma response protocol to provide immediate and comprehensive assistance to the employees, victims and families following a violent or traumatic event. Aside from immediate considerations like calling the police and obtaining emergency medical assistance, other issues will need to be addressed. It is important to identify who will calm witnesses, call victims' families, arrange transportation for victims, clean up damaged offices and grounds and talk to the press. Business interruptions are also inevitable. Preplanning the roles that various departments and personnel will take following a traumatic event can ease the impact, both practically and emotionally, that a critical incident can have on an organization and its employees.

Another important consideration is providing on-site debriefing/counseling services for employees and victims of a violent incident. As part of developing a trauma response protocol, professional counselors and psychologists should be identified as the debriefing team for the organization. The debriefing team should have specific and specialized training in trauma response in organizations, and have experience working with victims of violent crimes. This team will typically provide both group and individual debriefing meetings, and help facilitate access to ongoing psychotherapy for those who may need additional psychological assistance beyond the scope of the debriefing services. It is important to assess whether your debriefing group can provide counselors who match the cultural and language demographics of your employee population. For example, if your workforce is primarily made up of Hispanic, Spanish-speaking males, your debriefing team must be able to provide Hispanic, Spanish-speaking male therapists. Response time is also critically important. Determine how quickly your debriefing team can be onsite following an event. We recommend that they should be able to be present within 2-3 hours.

DISCUSSION QUESTIONS:

1. Does your organization have an established Critical Incident Plan? If so, what are the elements of that plan? Is the plan adequate?

2. Discuss the value of a Critical Incident Team and how it would be effective in preventing workplace violence. Is your Team trained periodically to maintain its readiness status?

3. Discuss the role of each member of a Critical Incident Team and apply those roles in your organization.

Chapter Seven
A Tool Kit to Address Potentially Violent Employees

The Critical Incident Assessment Team often calls upon the resources and expertise of other professional individuals and organizations. These resources, which we term the "tool kit" of the CIAT, can be important assets in managing potentially violent employees and in responding to critical incidents in the workplace. The following tools are available to the Critical Incident Assessment Team in managing potentially violent employees and situations. These tools are designed to achieve specific results and interventions. The key to the use of these tools is the judgment by the Critical Incident Assessment Team as to what would be effective, based on the individual circumstance and what risks are involved by using a particular tool at a particular point in time. It is important that the descriptions listed are for the purpose of education and do not to imply operational instructions. The reader should consult with qualified professionals in concert with the Critical Incident Assessment Team in using these tools.

Employee Assistance Program – EAPs assist employees whose work behavior may be adversely affected by personal or psychological problems. EAP counseling services are short-term, problem-focused interventions, which emphasize brief, counseling strategies that are solution oriented. This type of counseling emphasizes skills and strengths and encourages practicing new behaviors. Brief counseling also involves setting goals that are achievable in a one to five month period. Referrals to EAP are typically interventions designed to address psychological and performance problems as an early intervention in the Threat Assessment process.

Fitness-for-Duty Medical Exams This type of exam is typically requested by a company to determine if an employee has a mental condition, is potentially dangerous and is or is not fit to work. In the case of Fitness-for-duty exams, it is important to identify licensed psychologists, psychiatrists and physicians who have experience assessing mental and physical <u>disorders as they relate to the workplace</u>. These individuals, retained and paid for by the organization, are hired to assess the psychological or physical "fitness" of the employee; in other words, whether there is any condition, mental or physical, which would prevent the employee from safely fulfilling the requirements of their job position. They do not act as a therapist or personal physician for the employee; rather, their "client" is the organization. While there are many competent mental health professionals and physicians practicing today, it is crucial that the organization work with individuals with experience not only in their respective fields, but also in how companies function and in violence risk assessment in the workplace. This provider can also make recommendations about accommodating specific types of psychological disorders. The employee should not be returned to work until authorized to do so by the Fitness-for-duty provider.

There are essentially three types of professionals that are most likely retained for a Fitness-for-duty exam. These are psychologists, psychiatrists and general medical physicians. Psychologists can administer and interpret psychological testing in addition to conducting a clinical and historical interview with the employee. Psychiatrists can conduct a comprehensive clinical interview and assess any psychotropic medication issues that may be present. Physicians can assess whether there are any medical conditions that may be affecting job performance. In all cases, these providers must have experience with violence risk assessment *and* in working for organizations as a medical consultant. Additionally, before evaluating any employee in question, these providers should ask for and be provided a description of the essential functions of the employee's job. The service provider should also be provided any copies of performance evaluations and other documentation, which will describe job performance, interpersonal relationships at work, and previously attempted interventions, by the organization.

Involuntary Hospitalization (Cal-5150) – In California, individuals who are deemed a danger to themselves or to someone else can be held for evaluation in a hospital for up to 72 hours (Welfare and Institutions Code 5150). In most states, mental health providers and physicians are required to inform the authorities if a person is in imminent danger of hurting themselves or has made a threat of harm to another person. Typically, the police or a Psychiatric Emergency Team (PET) evaluates the person in question. If it is believed that the person is in fact a serious risk to himself or herself or someone else, that individual can be hospitalized for protection and evaluation. Medical practitioners and law enforcement agencies may use this tool; it is important to know the laws and regulations in your area.

Treatment – This is an intervention option provided by a mental health professional or physician. The treatment can consist of counseling, medications, or medical interventions. In some cases, the employer as a condition of employment may mandate treatment. Time off from work may be required to begin or establish treatment, particularly when substance abuse or psychosis is an issue.

Duty to Warn – A law that requires medical and mental health practitioners who are treating a patient who threatens to do harm to another person. In California, this is called the Tarasoff rule. The practitioner is obligated to warn the person(s) who is (are) the object of the threat that a threat has been made. In most states, they are also required to inform the police of the threat.

Temporary Restraining Orders (TRO) –A TRO's primary function is to legally restrain a person from interacting with another person or organization. The TRO is granted by the courts and specifies that an individual must not be within a certain distance of the other person or of the premises of an organization. In some states, like California, organizations as well as individuals may obtain a TRO. Most often, TROs are used if an employee, ex-employee or spouse/partner of an employee has made a threat against a person or against the organization as a whole. TROs can be effective in deterring some individuals from returning to the worksite. However, whenever the decision to obtain a TRO is considered, it is important to evaluate that decision carefully and obtain consultation with legal and psychological experts. The reason is that for some potentially violent individuals, a restraining order is a "triggering event." That is, it is the event that is the last straw and the one that provokes violent retaliation.

Assessment Meeting with the Potentially Violent Employee –The purpose of this meeting is to discuss the present concerns regarding workplace behavior, any threats which have been made or have been reported to have been made, and to gain information about potential risk factors for the employee. Only a trained Critical Incident Assessment Team member or Threat Assessment Specialist, such as a psychologist, should conduct this session.

Security – Employers are required by law to provide adequate security for their worksites. Security and related policies and procedures should be assessed regularly by management for familiarity and efficacy. Effective security procedures are designed to establish physical as well as procedural boundaries, which maximize the safety of the workplace and its employees. Electronic security systems are often added for mid to large size companies, and in cases of increased security risk. For companies with in-house security personnel, having a relationship with an outside security company to augment internal resources as needed is a valuable tool. For smaller companies without internal security departments, it is important to develop a relationship with a security provider prior to a crisis situation. Security in most cases should be non-uniformed, unobtrusive and, in some situations, armed.

Disability Retirement – This is an option that can humanely resolve a situation where an employee has been medically determined to be disabled and subsequently accepted for disability retirement. This ensures that the employee has some financial resources even though they are no longer working, potentially reducing the personal stressors that the individual may be experiencing. This option also provides the employee an opportunity to leave the organization with a sense of dignity and respect.

Separation Agreement – This kind of agreement can be a way in which the employee and the company can part in a mutually agreeable fashion. In typical cases, the employee agrees to resign in exchange for a severance package, continuation of benefits for a predetermined period of time, and outplacement. Sometimes, the organization agrees to provide a letter of reference verifying dates of employment and positions occupied. Again, this is an option which can potentially mitigate feelings of helplessness and lack of control, and provides financial and job-search resources for a period of time following the separation.

Safe Discharge – This option is essentially a strategic plan that is designed to reduce the risk that a potentially violent employee who has committed a dischargeable offense in the workplace does not carry out a violent act in retaliation for being fired. This typically involves consultation with experts from a variety of areas, including Threat Assessment Specialists, Legal, Security, EAP and Outplacement.

DISCUSSION QUESTIONS:

1. Does your organization offer an EAP? If so, how did you go choose your EAP provider? If not, what benefit would an EAP provide to your organization? Whether or not you currently have an EAP, what qualities do you think are most important in choosing a provider?

2. Under what circumstances might your organization refer someone for a "Fitness-for-duty" exam?

3. A Temporary Restraining Order (TRO) is sometimes used to prevent an individual from interacting with an organization. What do you think are some liabilities in pursuing a restraining order against a potentially violent employee? What are some of the benefits to the organization?

4. Who is your current security resource? What services can they provide to your organization? What services might you need in the futures that are not provided by this security company? Identify other resources, if necessary, to meet these needs.

Chapter Eight:

The Role of Employee Psychological Assessments in Workplace Violence Prevention

When there are concerns about an employee who has made a threat or who is behaving in an unusual, changed, bizarre or aggressive manner, two valuable tools to organizations in assessing risk and determining appropriate intervention steps are the Violence Risk Assessment and the Fitness-for-duty evaluation. Both of these tools provide a valuable window into the perspective and psychological functioning of the individual in question. Each of these interventions should be guided and conducted by experts in their respective fields. This chapter will focus on these two specific modes of evaluation and explore the roles that each of these can play in the assessment process. This chapter is intended as an overview, and not as advice for a given situation. Determination about the most appropriate assessment method for a particular circumstance should be made in concert with a threat assessment professional and a legal representative.

Violence Risk Assessment

After an employee has verbalized a threat or committed an aggressive act, a company will often feel paralyzed by concern about how to respond to the situation. On one hand, the organization has a duty to enforce company policy and maintain a safe working environment. On the other hand, the individuals to whom the threat has been reported are often fearful about "setting off" the person who was alleged to have made the threat or engaged in the hostile behavior. In the other extreme, some company officials can dismiss the threat entirely, stating something like "John would never do anything like that, he's just blowing off steam." In both cases, a thorough Violence Risk Assessment can provide valuable information in evaluating level of risk, and in guiding organizational response.

Very often, one of the first steps in violence risk assessment involves gathering information about the history of the employee at the organization. Included in this history is information about length of time with the company, job performance, relationships (including relationships with co-workers, subordinates and supervisors), attendance, leaves taken and any background of threats, aggressive behavior or policy violations. Additionally, as a part of this step of a violence risk assessment, obtain facts about any changes in the work environment (i.e., promotion, demotion, or a change in supervision), or anything about which an employee may be angry or resentful or otherwise emotionally charged. Often, personnel records are reviewed and relevant parties are interviewed to obtain as much information about the individual as possible. If a threat has been made or implied, information about the threat is gathered from witnesses to the threat or threatening action. It is not uncommon at this point to hire a security professional to conduct a background investigation, in an effort to determine whether this individual has a documented history of violent behavior (i.e., arrests or convictions for assault, rape or murder), as well as to determine whether the individual in question is a registered gun owner.

Interviewing the employee who has allegedly made the threat, or has allegedly displayed strange or unusual behavior, is another important step in violence risk assessment. During this phase of the risk assessment process, which may occur before or during the step described above (depending upon the immediacy of the situation), the individual should *be interviewed by an expert in threat assessment,* preferably with a background in psychology, psychiatry or a related mental health field. The threat assessment expert should be introduced to the employee by explaining that a threat was reported (or behavior on the part of the employee was reported as concerning) and that the expert was retained by the organization as a consultant to gather information and determine the safest way for the company to proceed.

As a part of the assessment process, the threat assessment expert will assess the relevant risk and stability factors for the individual. He or she will also determine if there are any diagnoses present, which may increase risk (i.e., depression, personality disorders, substance abuse) and approximate whether the employee has a **plan** to carry out a violent act, the **means** to commit an act of violence, and most importantly, the **intent** to carry out an act of violence. This information will be crucially important in determining the level of risk that the individual poses to the organization.

The degree to which employees cooperate with this process varies. Some are extremely compliant and provide all of the requested information. Others are highly angry or suspicious and refuse to participate at all. In each case, once either the interview is completed, or the individual has made it known that they refuse to cooperate, the employee is typically told that they are being placed on a leave of absence *with pay,* and that they are not to return to the premises until they are advised to do so by a designated individual. In some cases, particularly those in which the individual is non-cooperative, or hostile, or the level of risk appears moderate to high, it is appropriate to have security present to escort the individual off company grounds and to be present until the assessment process is complete.

After the threat assessment expert has interviewed the employee in question, and gathered the relevant background information, he or she will provide the organization with an estimate of the level of risk that the employee appears to pose to the organization or individuals within the organization. Based upon level of risk and upon specific information obtained about the organization and the relevant circumstances, recommendations are made about how to proceed, with the ultimate goal being to de-escalate the individual and protect all members of the organization from harm. These interventions can include termination, disciplinary action, mandatory EAP referral, organizational intervention, performance contracts, and written or verbal warnings regarding conduct. If termination is the ultimate outcome, then level of risk for acting out in reaction to termination can also be assessed, and security measures put into place during and following the termination meeting.

Not infrequently, based upon the outcome of the violence risk assessment, it is recommended that the individual undergo further in-depth assessment to determine if he or she is safe to be in the work environment. This type of evaluation is known as a Fitness-for-duty Evaluation.

Fitness-for-duty Evaluations

Often, upon completion of the threat assessment process, there is adequate information to indicate that the employee may pose a risk to the company. However, other times the information, which is gathered during this process, is incomplete or insufficient to make a specific determination about how to proceed. If it is the intention of the organization to retain the employee, a Fitness-for-duty exam is an appropriate option for assessing and intervening with the employee in question. If it is the intention of the organization to terminate or otherwise separate from the employee, then a Fitness-for-duty exam would not be appropriate, because the question of whether or not they can continue to work becomes a moot point.

Fitness-for-duty evaluations are psychological, psychiatric or physical exams which are conducted to determine whether an individual is "Fit for Duty" or able to meet the requirements of the job position from a technical and safety standpoint. This process involves an examination of the employee to assist the organization in understanding the risk, if any that may be posed to it, and whether it is appropriate to have the individual physically at the worksite. Fitness-for-duty evaluations are a valuable tool in determining organizational response to a threat or related concern.

There are typically three types of professionals you are most likely to retain for a Fitness-for-duty exam. These are psychologists, psychiatrists and physicians. Psychologists are trained to administer and interpret psychological testing in addition to conducting a clinical and historical interview with the employee; a psychiatrist can conduct a comprehensive clinical interview and assess any psychotropic medication issues that may be present; a physician can assess whether there are any medical or medication conditions that may be affecting job performance and conduct.

In all circumstances, when dealing with potential workplace violence, these providers must have experience with violence risk assessment *and* in working for organizations as a medical consultant. Additionally, before evaluating any employee in question, these providers should ask for and be provided a description of the essential functions of the employee's job. The service provider should also be provided any copies of performance evaluations and other documentation, which will describe job performance, interpersonal relationships at work, and previously attempted interventions, by the organization.

In cases of potential dangerousness, most companies make continued employment contingent on submission to the Fitness-for-duty exam. As we have mentioned, if a Fitness-for-duty evaluation is ordered for an employee, we strongly recommend that the employee be placed on a leave of absence *with pay* until the outcome of the evaluation is complete. This strategy keeps the potentially dangerous employee offsite until more is known about the degree of risk that is posed, and does not add to any potential financial stressors for the employee, which could serve to increase risk.

Typically, the employee, after being placed on a leave of absence, is informed that he or she must submit to a Fitness-for-duty examination. He or she is told where, and by whom, the exam will be conducted, and that he or she will be informed of the outcome after the organization has received the results. The employee will then report to the examination with the designated doctor, who will administer whatever tests and interviews are necessary to make a determination about job safety and potential dangerousness. The physician or psychologist in turn will provide the organization with a report detailing the results, and recommendations about whether or not the employee should be at the worksite ("Fit for Duty" or "Not Fit for Duty"). If the employee is deemed fit to return to the worksite, then the doctor may provide recommendations for the transition back to work. If it is determined that the employee should not be at work, then recommendations about what treatment the employee needs and an estimate of the amount of time the employee will need off to obtain treatment and stabilize the condition may also be detailed.

Fitness-for-duty evaluations provide documentation of problems and conditions, which may pose a threat to the workplace. Some

Human Resource and legal professionals can see this as a double-edged sword. On one hand, if an individual is assessed and a psychiatric or medical condition is identified, then the company may be obligated to provide accommodations to that employee under the Americans with Disabilities Act (ADA). On the other hand, if a condition exists and the organization chooses not to pursue assessing risk because of fear of falling under the jurisdiction of ADA, and facing the legal issues which accompany this, every employee and the organization as a whole is at risk. We prefer to think about this dilemma in the following way. The money an organization spends either accommodating an employee or legally defending themselves against an ADA claim is *miniscule* compared to the cost of human life, medical and legal expenses, business reputation and employee turnover, in the event of a tragic incident of violence. In protecting against a potentially violent employee, it is often a question of weighing the lesser of the two evils. Recent court rulings have recognized that ADA doesn't apply if there has been a legitimate threat against the organization and its' employees. But be sure to check with your legal counsel.

After receiving the Fitness-for-duty results, the organization can take the information from the violence risk assessment (if conducted) and compare it with the results from the Fitness-for-duty exam. Typically, consultation with legal resources follows, and a plan for how to proceed is developed. Fitness-for-duty exams, when utilized appropriately, can be invaluable in assessing risk and ultimately protecting the organization from a violent incident.

DISCUSSION QUESTIONS:

1. What kind of information is important in performing a violence risk assessment?

2. What are some factors that you think could influence the outcome of such an assessment?

3. What is important in choosing a provider to perform a Fitness-for-duty evaluation? In what kinds of situations are they typically performed? In what situation is it not appropriate to refer for this kind of exam?

4. Are there ADA concerns when requiring a Fitness-for-duty exam? If so, what are they?

Chapter Nine

A Menu of Security Measures

Security procedures are important to organizations of any size, industry and demographic makeup. Effective organizational security protects employees as well as customers, protects the organization from internal as well as external threats, and decreases the overall likelihood that the organization will be involved in a critical incident. Of course, it is impossible to have a workplace in which the security system is 100% effective in preventing any act of violence. Most organizations simply cannot have armed guards and metal detectors at every entrance. However, the more security elements an organization has in place, the less likely a potentially violent individual will be able to carry out a plan to commit a violent act.

Typically, when organizations have built-in security procedures and processes, the employees who work at those organizations feel more secure. Organizations send a message to their employees when they implement security procedures. When policies and procedures are a part of the day-to-day operations of the company, the message given to employees is that the organization is proactive in promoting safety and protection in the workplace. When security is "stepped up" following a threat or violent incident, the organization conveys its concern and its willingness to take these events seriously and respond accordingly. This can build employee loyalty and trust.

The list below represents a menu of security measures that should be considered when developing a security plan for any organization. The items below are not inclusive, and do not necessarily apply to all organizations at all times. It is suggested that an expert in industrial security be consulted when developing any new policies or procedures related to safety.

Parking Lot Lighting – Parking lots should be well-lit, and provide good visibility for those walking to and from their cars. Lighting should also be sufficient so that individuals can easily be seen from the interior of the building (i.e., from entrances and windows). All parking spaces should be at least 50 feet from any entrance. Very large parking lots or underground parking, with accessible panic buttons in the parking garage, are also suggested options. This assists in preventing an individual who is not authorized to be onsite from "slipping in" a door when someone else is leaving.

Metal Detectors – These types of devices can be installed to detect weapons such as guns, knives, artillery, and other potentially lethal weapons. They are used most often in very high crimes areas and in industries requiring a high degree of security such as airports and government offices. If metal detectors are used they need to be monitored by qualified security personnel at all times. Pre-determined response procedures need to be established and rehearsed prior to implementing this type of security procedure.

Bullet-resistant Glass – This type of security precaution is typically used in entrances to businesses and in areas where money is exchanged. Bullet-resistant glass is frequently used in high-crime areas.

113

Secured Lobbies – Lobbies, which are secured typically, have one locked entrance, which allows visitors to enter the facility after they have passed through the main lobby. After a visitor has identified himself/herself and signed in, the receptionist can then release the lock to allow the authorized individual to enter the facility. Some secured lobbies also have bullet-resistant glass to protect the receptionist.

"Call Buttons" for Receptionists – Discretely placed in the reception or customer service areas, this "panic button" will allow employees to summon help quickly in the case of an emergency. As a part of the call-button procedure, there should be a designated individual who responds to the call button when it is activated. Response procedures should also be clearly outlined and communicated.

Access Control Systems (Key Cards, Voice Identification) – Access control systems are a highly effective way of controlling access to a facility and give organizations the ability to monitor who has been entering and exiting the facility. Modern systems allow companies to activate and cancel access cards as needed, and also allow the organization to restrict access to certain areas or to certain individuals.

Employee Badges/Identification – Employees should be issued and required to wear photo identification cards at all times while on company property. This policy makes intruders and unauthorized visitors easier to identify. Badges are often combined with key cards, and should be taken immediately from any employee separating from the company at the time of separation.

Monitored Access Using Guard Services or Video Cameras – Additional monitoring of those who enter and exit a facility can be achieved by installing a guard at the entrance(s) of the building or by installing a closed-circuit video system in which a camera in the reception area can transmit video information to the security office of the facility.

Locking All Doors and Windows – Simply stated, all doors and windows should be locked from the inside, preventing access to unauthorized visitors and personnel. Doors should still allow for emergency exit.

Strictly Enforced Sign-In/Badge Procedures – Access to outsiders should be restricted. All visitors should be required to identify themselves and the reason for their visit to the facility. Visitors should be required to sign in when they arrive, and identify their contact within the company. Only those with official business with the organization should be allowed onsite, and then, only when accompanied by authorized personnel. Visitors should be required to wear a badge identifying themselves as visitors, and the badge should be surrendered upon leaving the company for the day. Visitors should also be required to sign out when they leave the premises for any reason, and sign in again when they return.

Enlist All Employees to Assist in Security Vigilance- During every new-hire orientation, employees should be advised of the specific policies relating to security and their obligations as employees of the company with regard to these policies. All employees should be instructed to report any unusual individual, activity or threats or threatening behavior to security and/or Human Resources immediately. Follow-up reminders should be given to employees periodically regarding these procedures. Emphasize the fact that security is every employee's concern.

Select Security People with Strong Interpersonal Skills- It has been said that the greatest weapon that a security or law enforcement individual has is between his or her ears. Simply providing a weapon or a uniform to an individual does not make them a competent security provider. Security providers must be able to interact effectively and in a non-threatening manner, with the intent to de-escalate the emotionally enraged or potentially violent individual. Receptionists and any other front-line personnel should also possess strong interpersonal skills and be trained in dealing with difficult or hostile individuals.

Temporary Security Enhancements During Periods of Concern – Contracting with outside security providers can enhance internal security during times of heightened concern about potential violence. It is important to develop these types of relationships before crises occur, rather than having to choose a provider you do not know in a time of great need, thus increasing potential risk and liability for the company.

Violence Vulnerability Audit – Every organization needs to consider developing a full safety audit on a regular basis. Areas to include in the audit are:

- Threat assessment protocol
- Evaluation of current policies and procedures
- Employee and manager attitudes
- Security systems
- Compliance with employment law
- Conflict resolution/Grievance procedures
- Supervisory skills
- Job design
- Physical layout of facility
- Current safety training programs
- Potential safety hazards
- Response readiness to potential critical incident

Although total security is never an absolute, the above measures can provide the hurdles that can deter an angry employee bent on a violent act.

DISCUSSION QUESTIONS:

1. Identify and discuss the security in your organization. Is it adequate to minimize the possibility of an occurrence of a violent act?

2. Identify the areas in your workplace that are most vulnerable to easy access by a disturbed ex-employee who is violent and determined to get even with the company.

3. Are your receptionists and security employees trained to take appropriate action if they encounter an individual or situation, which may present a threat to employees? What is their contingent plan?

4. Discuss the roles of employees in addressing security and potentially violent employees. Do they know where to report such individuals? Are employees required to wear security badges at all times while on the premises? Are employees admitting unauthorized people into the facility by allowing, "piggy backing" through the automated card access system?

Chapter Ten
Education and Training for Managers and Supervisors

Because the potential for violence in the workplace continues to increase across industries, it is essential for every organization to develop a strategic plan to address potential problems. This plan should be based upon an audit of current security strengths and vulnerabilities, and should include some process for *prediction* and *identification* of a potential problem as well as prevention of future incidents. The cornerstone of any solid prevention program includes comprehensive training of an organization's executives, supervisors and employees to identify and manage potentially violent situations. Quality training programs increase participants' sensitivity to clues that suggest that an employee may become dangerous; clues which may previously have been ignored or dismissed as unimportant. Thus, the goal of training is to *increase awareness.* Training also provides important information about current policies and procedures, and designates where employees and supervisors should report their observations and concerns.

All training should include information about the risk factors mentioned earlier in this book that are associated with violence. However, effective training will provide not only a "checklist" of risk factors, but also a deeper understanding for what work means to people today, and how the threat of job loss or instability can trigger violent behavior in certain types of individuals. This understanding will assist managers and others in taking the appropriate psychological steps, in addition to legal and security steps, to manage volatile individuals.

Training, particularly regarding "people issues," often is a low priority. It can be viewed as "fluffy" or "psychobabble" or as an unnecessary or supplemental service that is offered, or even required, of managers but that is not really the "important part" of the business. Some of this attitude, which we have seen to be prevalent across organizations, seems to come from past training experiences. However, much of the time it originates from the attitude of the leadership of the company toward these types of issues. With regard to workplace violence prevention, or any safety-related issue, training should be treated as a priority within the organization, and the message that the training is not only important, but also *crucial* to the safe operation of the company must come from the highest levels of the organization. Only then will managers, supervisors and others approach this issue with the seriousness and diligence that is required to establish and maintain a safe working environment.

What Should Training Programs Include?

As mentioned, training is a critical component of any prevention strategy. Of particular importance in establishing an educational program, and particularly a workplace violence prevention program, is understanding the essential elements of inclusive training. All employees, following the completion of training, should know how to report incidents of threatening, disruptive, bizarre, or assaultive behavior. Employees should also be provided a phone number that they can use for crises or emergencies. Supervisory training should emphasize the importance of a communicative and emotionally healthy work environment. Supervisors and managers should also be trained in how to set clear standards for performance, how to apply disciplinary measures, how to use employee meetings effectively, how to conduct performance counseling and the importance of addressing employee problems immediately. With the goal of training for workplace violence prevention being increased *awareness,* the following are core areas that should be addressed as a part of any effective program.

Threat Policy

Written policy statements are effective only to the degree that employees and managers are aware of the policies, and to the degree that they are consistently enforced within the organization. Although all employees should be informed of the threat policies of the organization during pre-hire orientation, and intermittently thereafter, workplace violence prevention training should be used to again communicate the policy. Included in the training related to the threat policy should be information regarding the kinds of behavior the policy covers, for instance, physical violence or assault and the possession or brandishing of a weapon. Non-physical violations of policy such as intimidation, harassment, threats or any behavior, which is intimidating or threatening to others, should also be discussed.

One of the most important things to be communicated during policy training is information regarding **where** and **how** employees, managers and supervisors should report policy violations. For instance, if an employee observes a co-worker threatening another person in the workplace, that employee should know to whom that behavior should be reported, that the behavior should be reported immediately, and that the report will be taken seriously and investigated promptly.

Warning Signs of Potentially Violent Employees

Training should provide employees with a basic understanding of the warning signs of potentially hostile or violent individuals. Included in this training can be examples of previous situations and perpetrators and a checklist of risk factors to be about which they need to be concerned. Employees should also be informed of the potential consequences of **not** reporting threats, changes in behavior or appearance, substance abuse or other observed warning signs. These consequences can include the actual occurrence of a violent incident, the perpetuation of a hostile and intimidating work environment, and in some cases, disciplinary action for not complying with a policy, which mandates that all employees report threatening types of behavior.

Early Intervention

A review of case studies of workplace violence perpetrators has established that many of these individuals demonstrated signs of difficulty or distress long before they acted out their frustration and anger against others. Most often, those around them were aware that the individual had been acting strangely, had decreased work performance, poor attendance or had verbalized threats, but no formal action had been taken by the company to intervene. We can only speculate about how early intervention with these employees may have produced very different kinds of outcomes. One of the keys to effective violence prevention is early intervention. Problems with employees need to be addressed while they are manageable. If problems are ignored, they are likely to only get bigger, sometimes to the point where a safety risk is created.

Training should place an emphasis on early intervention with potentially troubled employees. As mentioned earlier, intervention from co-workers will typically involve reporting an incident or change in behavior to a designated authority, who in turn further investigates and assesses risk. Managers will require specific training in how to intervene with employees; this can involve training in communication, stress management, EAP referral, defusing hostile situations and identifying violence prone employees, both during the interview process and post-hire. The importance of intervening at the <u>earliest possible level</u> should be underscored repeatedly.

Dealing With the Emotionally Charged and Enraged Employee

Training programs, particularly for managers and supervisors, must include instruction in how to deal with emotionally enraged and potentially dangerous employees. In addition to being able to recognize risk factors which may point to an increased risk for violence, managers must have the tools necessary to communicate "in the moment" with employees who are emotionally upset, frustrated, angry, and in some cases, making threats to harm themselves or someone else.

Instruction should include providing examples of the types of emotionally charged employees that they are most likely to encounter. Typically, employees who are upset are likely to be experiencing one of three types of emotions. The first is **frustration**. Many employees feel frustrated because they perceive that their concerns are not being heard, either by their supervisors or by the organization as a whole. Often, they are frustrated because they feel that some sort of unfair treatment has occurred. Sometimes, frustration that occurs at work compounds frustration that is ongoing at home, and the frustration is manifested in a variety of ways in the workplace. The second emotion that is commonly observed is **fear.** Employees who are having difficulties on the job are often fearful about losing their livelihood, economic security, and sense of identity; issues related to survival can become paramount. They may also be fearful of how important others view them if they lose their job. The third emotion is **anger,** and is manifested by the individual we call the "**emotionally enraged**" employee. This is the employee who experiences a great sense of rage, hostility and entitlement toward the organization, and has often escalated to the point where they view retaliation as the only option in dealing with their intense feelings. When anger reaches significant proportions, and when the individual has limited resources for coping or cannot identify alternatives, those who are emotionally enraged are typically the most dangerous, and should be approached cautiously.

Managers and supervisors should be trained to recognize the verbal and non-verbal signs of each of these emotional states, and should be given a basic understanding of the kinds of events and cognitions that contribute to emotional reactions on the part of their employees. They should receive specific instruction in conducting performance reviews and in addressing behavioral problems. Managers and supervisors should also be educated about the organizational factors (Chapter 4) so that they can be aware of, and move to correct, any factors in the work environment that could contribute to risk. Additionally, management training should include some very specific instruction on how to listen carefully to emotionally enraged employees, how to defuse, rather than escalate, emotionally charged situations, and how to respond to threats in the workplace. Management personnel need to know what resources are available to them in handling difficult employees (i.e., EAP, Human Resources, Security, etc.) and how to access those resources quickly and effectively. It is also important to discuss the importance of documentation of employee problems, and to provide examples of the legal and appropriate ways to keep record of an employee's performance across time.

Finally, it is important that management receive training in how to respond to employees following a violent incident. Management training programs should include modules, which provide information about the psychological impact of trauma, as well as rapid response personnel to assist in crisis intervention and debriefing. Training should also include procedures for monitoring individuals during emotional turmoil and recovery phases following trauma so that effective mental health referral can be made when necessary.

Crisis Procedures in Dealing With Immediate Situations

Ideally, every organization has a crisis response plan to address procedures and the roles of various individuals in the event of a crisis. Often, this plan has been designed by Human Resources, Security, Legal, and Risk Management or Loss Prevention Departments and involves a specific protocol that is to be followed when an emergency occurs. It is vitally important that crisis procedures be communicated to management personnel during training. Managers and supervisors should know who to call, if and when evacuation of the facility is appropriate, how information will be disseminated, and the role of the trauma response team following a critical incident. Information about these procedures should be clearly communicated in training and also be provided in workbook form for easy reference.

DISCUSSION QUESTIONS:

1. Why is training of managers so important? Why is training of employees so important? What is the primary goal of comprehensive training?

2. With regard to workplace violence, all training programs should include information about current policies and procedures. What are the policies and procedures with regard to workplace violence for your organization?

3. What are some barriers to providing effective training in your organization? What are some ideas for overcoming those barriers and still providing effective and comprehensive training programs?

4. What are some of the "emotionally enraged" behaviors that you have seen in your organization? What is the typical response to those behaviors? Is this response productive or counterproductive? What would you like to see happen differently?

Chapter Eleven
Legal Issues

As with any issue that an employer has to face, there are legal considerations that need to be addressed in any situation involving potentially violent employees. Obviously, legal precedents will vary from state to state, so the following is an overview of some of the most salient issues that are faced by employers. *This chapter is not intended as legal advice, and is not a substitute for contacting an attorney who specializes in employment law in your area of the country to help identify applicable statutes and regulations that may govern your organization.*

Negligent Hiring – This tort is based on the premise that an employer has a duty to protect its employees, contractors, customers, vendors and visitors from injuries caused by employees whom the employer knows, or should know, poses a risk of harm to others. This duty is breached when an employer fails to exercise reasonable care that its employees and customers are free from risk of harm caused by unfit employees. Thus, if an employer hires an employee who commits a violent act and the employer is aware or should have been aware that the employee has violent tendencies or had a violent past, the employer may be liable for any damages, which occurred as a result of the employee's actions. The risk of having to defend a claim based on negligent hiring is another reason to conduct thorough background and reference checks on all new employees.

Negligent Retention - This legal principal may apply when an employer **retains** an employee who has demonstrated violent tendencies or behavior in the workplace and yet the employer took no action or ineffective action to address the situation. An employer must take remedial steps to separate a violent or potentially violent employee from customers, vendors, contractors and other employees. Claims under this theory commonly result from situations in which a violent incident occurred and the employer had direct or indirect knowledge of threats or threatening behavior on the part of an employee, but chose to ignore or work around the individual rather than taking steps to assess and intervene appropriately.

Negligent Supervision – The theory of negligent supervision asserts that the employer should take "reasonable care" in supervising an employee who is threatening another employee with violent behavior. If "reasonable care" in controlling, monitoring or supervising the employee is not taken, and a violent incident occurs, the company may be held liable.

American Disabilities Act – The Americans with Disabilities Act ("ADA") prohibits discrimination against qualified individuals with a disability, regardless of whether the employer receives federal funds, and regardless of whether the disability is mental or physical. The ADA requires employers to provide *reasonable accommodation* for qualified employees who have a physical or mental disability in order to maintain their employment. In the context of violent behavior, where it has been determined that the employee is mentally ill, the question that often arises is "is the employer required to reasonably accommodate this violent or potentially violent employee?" Generally, the answer is "no." In most circumstances the employer is free to take the appropriate remedial steps, including disciplinary action, in order to ensure that other employees can work in an environment free from the risk of harm.

Chapter 11

Privacy Act – Various laws and regulations prohibit or protect the release of information regarding individuals, including information pertaining to applicants, employees and former employees. These records might include information related to prior employment or medical records. As a general matter employers are free to seek whatever information is lawfully available concerning applicants, including prior criminal records. However, with regard to an employer's obligation to provide prospective employers with information concerning the violent tendencies of individuals, the law is in a state of flux. In some jurisdictions the courts have found that an employer is free to limit the information provided to dates of employment and positions held. Other courts have held that once an employer provides *any* information beyond simply dates and positions, the employer is obligated to provide *all* of the relevant information, including information that might touch an individual's violent tendencies.

The release of medical information, including psychiatric or psychological evaluations, must also be handled with extreme care and through appropriate medical sources. As a general rule, current employees, as well as applicants and former employees have a legitimate expectation of privacy for their medical records. The "need to know" is a critical standard in gaining information related to medical conditions. Such information is in many cases a critical part of a Threat Assessment process. When obtaining any confidential information in the Threat Assessment process care must be taken to preserve, to the greatest extent possible, the privacy rights of the individual in question.

Occupational Safety & Health Act (OSHA) –An employer who learns that a current or former employee has threatened violence against others in the workplace may be required to take certain preventative steps under the Federal Occupational Safety and Health Act (Fed/OSHA) statutory scheme. The General Duty Clause requires that employers provide their employees with a workplace that is "free from recognizable hazards that are causing or are likely to cause death or serious physical harm…to employees." There are two critical OSHA requirements employers must consider. First, an employer must provide a safe and healthy working environment for their employees. Secondly, **Fed/OSHA has issued guidelines** to assist employers in complying with the General Duty Clause to provide a safe work environment. These guidelines are not standards or regulations and are advisory in nature only. However, it is also important to note that Fed-OSHA will rely on the General Duty Clause for enforcement authority. The guidelines state that "employers can be cited for violating the General Duty Clause if there is a recognized hazard of workplace violence in their establishments and they do nothing to prevent or abate it." Failure to implement the guidelines is not in and of itself a violation of the General Duty Clause; however, failure to provide a safe working environment, especially with knowledge of a workplace violence threat, can be.

DISCUSSION QUESTIONS:

1. Discuss the obligations of your organization under the Occupational Safety & Health Act (OSHA) to maintain a safe work environment. What processes are in place in your organization, which comply with the OSHA guidelines to prevent violence?

2. Who in your organization has access to employee medical records? Is that person on the Threat Assessment Team? Why or why not?

3. Discuss the circumstances when an organization can be successfully sued in workplace violence situations.

References

American Psychiatric Association: *Diagnostic and Statistical Manual of Mental Disorders*,
  Fourth Edition. Washington, DC, American Psychiatric Association, 1994.

Aversa, J. *Violence Still Saturates Television, Study Reports.* San Jose Mercury News, April 16,
  1998.

Baron, S.A. (1993). Violence in the Workplace: A Prevention and Management Guide for
  Businesses. Ventura, CA: Pathfinder Publishing.

Baron, S.A. (1994). Violence in Our Schools, Hospitals and Public Places: A Prevention and
  Management Guide. Ventura, CA: Pathfinder Publishing.

Bureau of Justice Statistics. (1998) National Crime Victimization Survey: Workplace Violence
  1992-1996.

California Occupational Safety and Hazard Act (CAL/OSHA). *Guidelines for Workplace
  Security.* California Department of Industrial Relations, Division of Occupational Safety and
  Health.

Cawood, J.S. (1991). *On the Edge: Assessing the Violent Employee.* Security Management

Magazine.

Kinney, J.A., & Johnson, D.L. (1993). <u>Breaking Point: The Workplace Violence Epidemic and</u>
   <u>What to Do About It</u>. Chicago: National Safe Workplace Institute.

Roizen, J. (1997). *Epidemiological Issues in Alcohol-Related Violence*. In: Galanter, M., ed.

   <u>Recent Developments in Alcoholism</u>. Vol 13, (pp 7-40). New York: Plenum Press.

U.S. Bureau of Labor Statistics, U.S. Department of Labor. National Census of Fatal
   Occupational Injuries, 1996.

U.S. Bureau of Labor Statistics, U.S. Department of Labor. Fatal Occupational Injuries by Event
   or Exposure, 1992-1997.

Workplace Violence Research Institute. (1994). <u>The Complete Workplace Violence Prevention</u>
   <u>Manual.</u>

APPENDIX A

CORPORATE CRISIS MANAGE-MENT PLAN

DATE

RESTRICTED

CORPORATE CRISIS MANAGEMENT PLAN

Phases

For purposes of this plan, there are three distinct phases in a crisis:

The pre-crisis, the crisis and the post-crisis phases.

Definitions

The pre-crisis phase is defined as any probable prelude to a crisis situation. Examples of warning signs and/or incidents that could lead to a crisis situation include, but are not limited to:

* Threats   * Excessive belligerence
* Outbursts   * Frequent arguments
* Bizarre physical actions   * Refusing to comply
                               with rules
* Bizarre expressed thoughts * Obsessions
* Sabotage   * Vandalism

A crisis is defined as a situation that has reached a critical phase and that severely impacts our normal operational procedures. It most likely is a traumatic event or tragic situation that directly impacts the lives and attitudes of our employees. Examples of crises include, but are not limited to:

* Suicide   * Robbery
* Murder   * Assault
* Natural Disaster   * Hostage-taking

The post-crisis phase is defined as that period after a crisis where the emotional and mental well being of employees precludes normal operational procedures.

Purpose

This plan is designed to mitigate the possibility that a pre-crisis situation will escalate into a crisis and to address the important physical and psychological consequences as a result of a tragic and/or traumatic event. Because of the multiple possibilities related to a crisis situation, this plan provides only the minimum essential elements and must not be interpreted as all-inclusive. As a situation unfolds, this plan should be expanded to include all specific actions necessary for resolving or alleviating any resultant impact on our employees and their families. Their well-being must remain paramount. In addition, the Crisis Team will develop specific responsibilities for each member.

PRE-CRISIS

Early Intervention

Experts agree that one significant key to preventing a pre-crisis incident from escalating into a crisis situation is quick intervention. Any delay in addressing the incident may confuse an already unstable employee and send a message that such behavior is acceptable or the delay may allow the individual to take further advantage of the situation.

Notification Protocols

Protocols to be followed if the incident appears likely to result in imminent danger, i.e., likelihood of assault accompanied by a high emotional state, inappropriate gestures, erratic or boisterous behaviors.

A.   Contact the local police (911) and the Security Office (Telephone Number.). Under no circumstances attempt to physically remove the individual from the office.

B.   Contact the *Crisis Manager* (Phone No.) and apprise him/her of the situation.

C.   Safeguard other employees, as warranted.

Protocols to be followed in stabilizing a situation in which there appears to be no imminent danger include:

A.   If able to resolve the situation without incident, do so. If the circumstances do not allow for self action, then

B.   Contact the Police/Security Office (Phone No.) and apprise them of the situation.

C.   Contact the *Crisis Manager* (Phone No.) and apprise him/her of the situation.

D.   Separate the employees involved and isolate them until interviewed.

E.   Obtain witness names and written statements sufficient to establish the circumstances leading to the incident.

To re-emphasize, employees are not expected to put themselves in a confrontational situation; if individuals are not willing to cooperate call the Security Office and *Crisis Manager*.

It is also imperative to emphasize that voice mail notification is not sufficient; personal notification must be made.

Critical Incident Assessment Team
Following notice of a pre-crisis incident, the *Crisis Manager* will assemble the Critical Incident Assessment Team consisting of the following (as appropriate):

Name   Office No.   Home No.
Human Resources VP/Manager
Security Officer
Legal Counsel
Employee Relations/Labor Relations

Appendix A
Medical Practitioner
EAP Counselor
Safety Professional
Line Manager
Professional Threat Assessment Specialist
Other Management as Appropriate

In the absence of the VP/Manager of Human Resources, the Crisis Manager will be (Name), followed by (Name).

The Critical Incident Assessment Team will confer with professional consultation resources/professionals to determine if there is a need for further action or mere monitoring of the situation. (Addendum "A" contains names and phone numbers of professionals who have agreed to assist in threat assessment or to provide counseling following a crisis situation.) The assessment phase consists of the following three components:

A. Initial Assessment
The team may interview the victim and/or witnesses/ targets to assess threat specifics, interpersonal dynamics, motivations and violence potential versus degree of impulse. An incident chronology will also be developed. Tests to determine if an actual threat occurred include:
* Body language and tone of voice.
* Employee's present ability to carry out the threat.
* Employee's propensity to engage in physical violence.
* Triggering event causing the employee to react.
* Context in which words were used by the employee.
* Response and reaction of the target.
* Employee's subsequent conduct, e.g., remorse, concern, desire to correct.

Following the analysis of this initial information, a decision will be made as to whether further action is warranted.

If further action is deemed appropriate, the next step is to conduct an in-depth background review.

B. In-depth Background Review

This segment of the assessment phase includes identifying any prior incidents as well as identifying any current "turbulence," e.g., employee evaluations, debts, legal problems, personal problems, etc. Sources of this information are obtained from personnel documents, e.g., Official Personnel Folder, Official Medical Folder, merit evaluations/manager's files, etc. Questions to be asked and facts to be determined include, but are not limited to:

Official Personnel Folder

1. Erratic/short term prior employment.
2. Unexplained periods of unemployment.
3. Reasons for leaving past employment, e.g., personality differences,
    health, stress, supervisor unfair/discrimination, harassment, no reason.
4. Problems during the military such as separation other than honorable and/or
    time deductions.
5. Receipt and basis of disability.

Official Medical File

1. History of behavioral problems.
2. Prior psychiatric fitness-for-duty examination.
3. History of absences due to stress and/or other emotional problems.

Evaluations/Manager's Files

1. Erratic or strange behaviors/work problems.
2. Attendance problems.
3. Disciplinary actions.

Other sources include co-worker interviews (extreme discretion must be used as this is very sensitive and can trigger privacy issues). It may also be advisable to determine a past history of relations with other employees and managers. Finally, outside sources include public records, financial records (if allowed) and/or weapons registration.

C. Final Assessment and Recommendations

Recommended actions will be developed for the purposes of defusing the situation and avoiding future problems. Recommendations may include scheduling for a fitness-for-duty examination, referring to EAP counseling, disciplining, referring to law enforcement agencies, implementing security plans. In addition, victims and/or targets will be given appropriate feedback information and support. The team will monitor and assign responsibility for implementation of recommendations and other actions.

CRISIS

During the time in which a crisis is actually happening, the foremost responsibility of any actively involved employee is the self-preservation of life where prudent and reasonable. Since this phase is dependent on the wide variety of circumstances, prior preparation to the extent possible will minimize the threat to life and injury. Prearranged security plans, evacuation plans and emergency police contact are critical components.

POST-CRISIS

Crisis Notifications

The Vice President or Manager of Human Resources, as the designated *Crisis Manager*, is responsible for ensuring that all affected organizations and parties are kept informed of the critical events and issues.

Upon notification of a crisis situation, the *Crisis Manager* will notify Emergency Response Team (ERT) members of the crisis as well as the (Name of Organization Leader) The *Crisis Manager* will also ensure the preparation of a preliminary report that is to be faxed to the (Name of Appropriate Management Employees) as soon as possible, but no later than 24 hours from the beginning of the crisis. *The Crisis Manager* and the Manager of Communications, will be the officials directly responsible for the confirmation of facts prior to the release of all official correspondence and communication from the organization involved either directly or indirectly with the crisis situation.

ERT Composition and Telephone Numbers

To react to situations quickly, the *Crisis Manager* will identify individuals who are responsible for the administration of the following:
* Care of injured employees and their families
* Safety and welfare of Company employees and the public
* Administration of benefits for victims and their families

Immediately upon notification of a crisis situation, the *Crisis Manager* will convene a meeting, if possible, of the ERT. In the event a meeting cannot be convened immediately, each team member is responsible for controlling his or her specific area of responsibility and conferring with the *Crisis Manager* at the earliest possible time. Meetings will reconvene every several hours to review restoration progress.

Name   Office   Home

Human Resources VP/Manager
Line Manager
Finance VP/Manager

Appendix A

Security Officer
Legal Counsel
Manager, Communications
Manager, Facilities
Manager, Employment/HRIS
Medical Practitioner
EAP Counselors (Crisis Specialists)
Other Sources as Designated

A briefing of the situation will be conducted and a complete review of the following guidelines will be conducted. Additional specific duties and responsibilities will be assigned to those present. The term "primary," listed next to a functional title, represents that individual or designee who has the direct responsibility for ensuring that a specific task is completed in the best interest of the Company and its employees.

Care of Affected Employees - ERT Responsibilities

1. In the event of severe injury or fatality, notification should be made in person to a family member by an executive, if at all possible.
   Responsible Officials: (A Senior Manager/Executive)

2. Take a head count of employees to ensure that all are accounted for.
   Responsible Officials: (Senior Managers) or designees (primary).

3. Arrange for sufficient immediate psychological counseling as needed. Determine the need for assigning victim/family counselors and the need to establish a counseling information telephone hotline. The intervention team should be onsite within two hours.
   Responsible Officials: Medical Practitioner (primary) and Human Resources.

4. Determine the need for, or assist in arranging medical care, consistent with workers' compensation requirements and company policy.
   Responsible Officials: Medical Practitioner (primary)
   Human Resources

5. Obtain accurate information concerning the extent of injuries (from medical source only), location of the hospital to which any employees
   have been taken, etc.
   Responsible Officials: Medical Practitioner (primary)
   Human Resources

6. Determine the family, employee's immediate needs (e.g., benefits, financial, etc.).
   Responsible Officials: Manager, Finance (primary)
   Human Resources (Personnel - primary)

7. Determine the need for authorizing administrative leave to those employees directly involved in the situation.
   Responsible Officials: Designated Manager, (primary)
   VP/Manager, Human Resources

8. Ensure that managers receive professional orientation and guidance on how to deal with employees who are the victims of shock or trauma.
   Responsible Officials: Medical Practitioner (primary)
   Human Resources
   EAP Counselors

9. Determine the need for providing meals to those remaining onsite.
   Responsible Officials: Designated Manager (primary)

Appendix A

<u>Safety of Employees and Public - ERT Responsibilities</u>
1. Ensure that appropriate action/evacuation plans have been activated.
    Responsible Officials: Human Resources (Safety - primary)
    Manager, Facility (primary)
    Local, State and Federal Officials

2. Determine the need for cleanup, repair and restoration.
    Responsible Officials: Manager, Facilities (primary)

3. Determine the need for coordination/contact with Fire Department personnel, OSHA, EPA.
    Responsible Officials: Human Resources (Safety - primary)
    Environmental Coordinator

4. Coordinate crime scene/facility access for response personnel with law enforcement officials.
    Responsible Officials: Security Officer (primary)

5. Ensure that sufficient and appropriate information is shared with employees and the public.
    Responsible Officials: Manager,Communications (primary)
    VP/Manager, Human Resources

6. Establish alternate work sites for employees and response personnel, as needed, including necessary support such as cellular phones, telephone lines, faxes, word processors.
    Responsible Officials: Manager, Facility (primary)

7. Contact and share information with appropriate company officials and unions .

142

Responsible Officials: VP/ Manager, Human Resources
(primary)
Manager Communications

Administration of Benefits - ERT Responsibilities

1.   Designate one person to each family as the Company contact who will coordinate all benefits for family or individuals.
Responsible Officials: Human Resources (primary)

2.   Establish expedited processing system and maintain regular contact with   those in other organizations (i.e. Life Insurance, Workers' Compensation, OSHA, Veterans' Administration, Social Security) who are processing claims until all benefits have been obtained.
Responsible Officials: Human Resources (Personnel - primary)

Communications Role

Communications will coordinate the release of information to the media related to the crisis. It is imperative that all information, proposed action and follow-up be coordinated with the *Crisis Manager*.

Security Officer's Role

The security officer and other designated management officials are responsible to conduct thorough investigations and assure adequate protection of company interests during the post-crisis period. The *Crisis Manager*, with the assistance of other "primary" designated officials, should keep the Security Officer fully apprised of all actions taken or contemplated. There must be particular attention to this liaison where circumstances involve criminal activity or serious hazard to employees or patrons.

APPENDIX B

CAL/OSHA GUIDELINES FOR SECURITY

OSHA VOLUNTARY GUIDELINES ON PREVENTING WORKPLACE VIOLENCE

The following are excerpts from the Occupational Safety and Health Act
Guidelines on Preventing Workplace Violence

Notice

These guidelines are not a new standard or regulation. They are advisory in nature, informational in content, and are intended for use by employers seeking to provide a safe and healthful workplace through effective workplace violence prevention programs adapted to the needs and resources of each place of employment. The guidelines are not intended to address issues related to patient care. The guidelines are performance-oriented and the implementation of the recommendations will be different, based upon an establishment's hazard analysis.

Violence inflicted upon employees may come from many sources – i.e., patients, third parties such as robbers or muggers – and may include co-worker violence. These guidelines address only the violence inflicted by patients or clients against staff. It is suggested, however, that workplace violence policies indicate a zero-tolerance for violence of any kind.

The Occupational Safety and Health Act of 1970 (OSH Act) mandates that, in addition to compliance with hazard-specific standards, all employers have a general duty to provide their employees with a workplace free from recognized hazards likely to cause death or serious physical harm. OSHA will rely on Section 5(a) of the OSH Act, the "General Duty Clause," for enforcement authority. Employers can be cited for violating the General Duty Clause if there is a recognized hazard of workplace violence in their establishments and they do nothing to prevent or abate it. Failure to implement these guidelines is not in itself a violation of the General Duty Clause of the OSH Act. OSHA will not cite employers who have effectively implemented these guidelines.

Further, when Congress passed the OSH Act, it did so based on a finding that job-related illnesses and injuries were imposing both a hindrance and a substantial burden upon interstate commerce, "in terms of lost production, wage loss, medical expenses, and disability compensation payments."

At the same time, Congress was mindful of the fact that workers' compensation systems provided state-specific remedies for job-related injuries and illnesses. Issues on what constitutes a compensable claim and what the rate of compensation should be were left up to the states, their legislatures, and their courts to determine. Congress acknowledged this point in Section 4(b)(4) of the OSH Act, when it stated categorically: "Nothing in this chapter shall be construed to supersede or in any manner affect any workmen's compensation law . . . ." Therefore, these non-mandatory guidelines should not be viewed as enlarging or diminishing the scope of work-related injuries and are intended for use in any state and without regard to whether the injuries or fatalities, if any, are later deemed to be compensable.

Appendix B

Acknowledgments

Many person, including health care, social services, and employee assistance experts; researchers, educators, unions, and other stakeholders; OSHA professionals; and the National Institute for Occupational Safety and Health (NIOSH) contributed to these guidelines.

Also, several states have developed relevant standards or recommendations, such as the California OSHA (CAL/OSHA), CAL/OSHA *Guidelines for Workplace Security*, and *Guidelines for Security* and *Safety of Health Care and Community Service Workers*; the Joint Commission on Accreditation of Health Care Organizations, *1995 Accreditation Manuals for Hospitals*; Metropolitan Chicago Healthcare Council, *Guidelines for Dealing with Violence in Health Care*; New Jersey Public Employees Occupational Safety and Health (PEOSH), *Guidelines on Measure and Safeguards in Dealing with Violent or Aggressive Behavior in Public Sector Health Care Facilities*; and the State of Washington Department of Labor and Industries, *Violence in Washington Workplaces*, and *Study of Assaults on Staff in Washington State Psychiatric Hospitals*. Information is available from these and other agencies to assist employers.

Introduction

For many years, health care and social service workers have faced a significant risk of job-related violence. Assaults represent a serious safety and health hazard for these industries, and violence against their employees continues to increase.

OSHA's new violence prevention guidelines provide the agency's recommendations for reducing workplace violence developed following a careful review of workplace violence studies, public and private violence prevention programs, and consultations with, and input from, stakeholders.

146

OSHA encourages employers to establish violence prevention programs and to track their progress in reducing work-related assaults. Although not every incident can be prevented, many can, and the severity of injuries sustained by employees reduced. Adopting practical measures such as those outlined here can significantly reduce this serious threat to worker safety.

OSHA's Commitment

The publication and distribution of these guidelines is OSHA's first step in assisting health care and social service employers and providers in preventing workplace violence. OSHA plans to conduct a coordinated effort consisting of research, information, training, cooperative programs, and appropriate enforcement to accomplish this goal.

The guidelines are not a new standard or regulation. They are advisory in nature, informational in content, and intended for use by employers in providing a safe and healthful workplace through effective violence prevention programs, adapted to the needs and resources of each place of employment.

Extent of Problem

Today, more assaults occur in the health care and social services industries than in any other. For example, Bureau of Labor Statistics (BLS) data for 1993 showed health care and social service workers have the highest incidence of assault injuries (BLS, 1993). Almost two-thirds of the nonfatal assaults occurred in nursing homes, hospitals, and establishments providing residential care and other social services (Toscano and Weber, 1995).

Assaults against workers in the health professions are not new. According to one study (Goodman et al., 1994), between 1980 and 1990, 106 occupational violence-related deaths occurred among the following health care workers: 27 pharmacists, 26 physicians, 18 registered nurses, 17 nurses' aides, and 18 health care workers in other occupational categories. Using the National Traumatic Occupational Fatality database, the study reported that between 1983 and 1989, there were 69 registered nurses killed at work. Homicide was the leading cause of traumatic occupational death among employees in nursing homes and personal care facilities.

A 1989 report (Carmel and Hunter) found that the nursing staff at a psychiatric hospital sustained 16 assaults per 100 employees per year. This rate, which includes any assault-related injuries, compares with 8.3 injuries of all types per 100 full-time workers in all industries and 14.2 per 100 full-time workers in the construction industry (BLS, 1991). Of 121 psychiatric hospital workers sustaining 134 injuries, 43 percent involved lost time from work with 13 percent of those injured missing more than 21 days from work.

Of greater concern is the likely underreporting of violence and a persistent perception within the health care industry that assaults are part of the job. Underreporting may reflect a lack of institutional reporting policies, employee beliefs that reporting will not benefit them, or employee fears that employers may deem assaults the result of employee negligence or poor job performance.

Risk Factors

Health care and social service workers face an increased risk of work-related assaults stemming from several factors, including:

♦ The prevalence of handguns and other weapons – as high as 25 %[5] – among patients, their families, or friends. The increasing use of hospitals by police and the criminal justice systems for criminal holds and the care of acutely disturbed, violent individuals.

♦ The increasing number of acute and chronically mentally ill patients now being released from hospitals without follow-up care, who now have the right to refuse medicine and who can no longer be hospitalized involuntarily unless they pose an immediate threat to themselves or others.

♦ The availability of drugs or money at hospitals, clinics, and pharmacies, making them likely robbery targets.

♦ Situational and circumstantial factors such as unrestricted movement of the public in clinics and hospitals; the increasing presence of gang members, drug or alcohol abusers, trauma patients, or distraught family members; long waits in emergency or clinic areas, leading to client frustration over an inability to obtain needed services promptly.

♦ Low staffing levels during times of specific increased activity such as meal times, visiting times, and when staff are transporting patients.

♦ Isolated work with clients during examinations or treatment.

♦ Solo work, often in remote locations, particularly in high-crime settings, with no back-up or means of obtaining assistance such as communication devices or alarm systems.

♦ Lack of training of staff in recognizing and managing escalating hostile and assaultive behavior.

♦ Poorly lighted parking areas.

Overview of Guidelines

In January 1989, OSHA published voluntary, generic safety and health program management guidelines for all employers to use as a foundation for their safety and health programs, which can include a workplace violence prevent ional program.[6] OSHA's violence prevention guidelines build on the 1989 generic guidelines by identifying common risk factors and describing some feasible solutions. Although not exhaustive, the new workplace violence guidelines include policy recommendations and practical corrective methods to help prevent and mitigate the effects of workplace violence.

The goal is to eliminate or reduce worker exposure to conditions that lead to death or injury from violence by implementing effective security devices and administrative work practices, among other control measures.

The guidelines cover a broad spectrum of workers who provide health care and social services in psychiatric facilities, hospital emergency departments, community mental health clinics, drug abuse treatment clinics, pharmacies, community care facilities, and long-term care facilities. They include physicians, registered nurses, pharmacists, nurse practitioners, physicians' assistants, nurses' aides, therapists, technicians, public health nurses, home health care workers, social/welfare workers, and emergency medical care personnel. Further, the guidelines may be useful in reducing risks for ancillary personnel such as maintenance, dietary, clerical, and security staff employed in the health care and social services industries.

Violence Prevention Program Elements

There are four main components to any effective safety and health program that also apply to preventing workplace violence: (1) management commitment and employee involvement, (2) worksite analysis, (3) hazard prevention and control, and (4) safety and health training.

Management Commitment and Employee Involvement

Management commitment and employee involvement are complementary and essential elements of an effective safety and health program. To ensure an effective program, management and front-line employees must work together, perhaps through a team or committee approach. If employers opt for this strategy, they must be careful to comply with the applicable provisions of the National Relations Act.[7]

Management commitment, including the endorsement and visible involvement of top management, provides the motivation and resources to deal effectively with workplace violence, and should include the following:

◆ Demonstrated organizational concern for employee emotional and physical safety and health.
◆ Equal commitment to worker safety and health and patient/ client safety.
◆ Assigned responsibility for the various aspects for the workplace violence prevention program to ensure that all managers, supervisors, and employees understand their obligations.
◆ Appropriate allocation of authority and resources to all responsible parties.
◆ A system of accountability for involved managers, supervisors and employees.
◆ A comprehensive program of medical and psychological counseling and debriefing for employees experiencing or witnessing assaults and other violent incidents.
◆ Commitment to support and implement appropriate recommendations from safety and health committees.

Employee involvement and feedback enable workers to develop and express their own commitment to safety and health and provide useful information to design, implement, and evaluate the program. Employee involvement should include the following:

◆ Understanding and complying with the workplace violence prevention program and other safety and security measures.
◆ Participation in an employee complaint or suggestion procedure covering safety and security concerns.
◆ Prompt and accurate reporting of violent incidents.
◆ Participation on safety and health committees or teams that receive reports of violent incidents or security problems, make

facility inspections, and respond with recommendations for corrective strategies.

♦ Taking part in a continuing education program that covers techniques to recognize escalating agitation, assaultive behavior, or criminal intent, and discusses appropriate responses.

Written Programs

A written program for job safety and security, incorporated into the organization's overall safety and health program, offers an effective approach for larger organizations. In smaller establishments, the program need not be written or heavily documented to be satisfactory. What is needed are clear goals and objectives to prevent workplace violence suitable for the size and complexity of the workplace operation and adaptable to specific situations in each establishment.

The prevention program and startup date must be communicated to all employees. At a minimum, workplace violence prevention programs should do the following:

♦ Create and disseminate a clear policy of zero-tolerance for workplace violence, verbal and nonverbal threats, and related actions. Managers, supervisors, co-workers, clients, patients, and visitors must be advised of this policy.

♦ Ensure that no reprisals are taken against an employee who reports or experiences workplace violence.[8]

♦ Encourage employees to promptly report incidents and to suggest ways to reduce or eliminate risks. Require records of incidents to assess risk and to measure progress.

♦ Outline a comprehensive plan for maintaining security in the workplace, which includes establishing a liaison with law enforcement representatives and others who can help identify ways to prevent and mitigate workplace violence.

♦ Assign responsibility and authority for the program to

individuals or teams with appropriate training and skills. The written plan should ensure that there are adequate resources available for this effort and that the team or responsible individuals develop expertise on workplace violence prevention in health care and social services.

♦ Affirm management commitment to a worker-supportive environment that places as much importance on employee safety and health as on serving the patient or client.

♦ Set up a company briefing as part of the initial effort to address such issues as preserving safety, supporting affected employees, and facilitating recovery.

Worksite Analysis

Worksite analysis involves a step-by-step, common-sense look at the workplace to find existing or potential hazards for workplace violence. This entails reviewing specific procedures or operations that contribute to hazards and specific locales where hazards may develop.

A "Threat Assessment Team," "Patient Assault Team," similar task force, or coordinator may assess the vulnerability to workplace violence and determine the appropriate preventive actions to be taken. Implementing the workplace violence prevention program then may be assigned to this group. The team should include representatives from senior management, operations, employee assistance, security, occupational safety and health, legal, and human resources staff.

The team or coordinator can review injury and illness records and workers' compensation claims to identify patterns of assaults that could be prevented by workplace adaptation, procedural changes, or employee training. As the team or coordinator identifies appropriate controls, these should be instituted.

Appendix B

The recommended program for worksite analysis includes, but is not limited to, analyzing and tracking records, monitoring trends and analyzing incidents, screening surveys, and analyzing workplace security.

Records Analysis and Tracking

The activity should include reviewing medical, safety, workers' compensation and insurance records – including the OSHA 200 log, if required – to pinpoint instances of workplace violence. Scan unit logs and employee and police reports of incidents or near-incidents of assaultive behavior to identify and analyze trends in assaults relative to particular departments, units, job titles, unit activities, work stations, and/or time of day. Tabulate these data to target the frequency and severity of incidents to establish a baseline for measuring improvement.

Monitoring Trends and Analyzing Incidents

Contacting similar local businesses, trade associations, and community and civic groups is one way to learn about their experiences with workplace violence and to help identify trends. Use several years of data, if possible, to trace trends of injuries and incidents of actual or potential workplace violence.

Screening Surveys

One important screening tool is to give employees a questionnaire or survey to get their ideas on the potential for violent incidents and to identify or confirm the need for improved security measures. Detailed baseline screening surveys can help pinpoint tasks that put employees at risk. Periodic surveys – conducted at least annually or whenever operations change or incidents of workplace violence occur – help identify new or previously unnoticed risk factors and deficiencies or failures in work practices, procedures, or controls. Also, the surveys help assess the effects of changes in the work processes (see Appendix A for a sample survey used in the State of Washington). The periodic review process should also include feedback and follow-up.

Independent reviewers, such as safety and health professionals, law enforcement or security specialists, insurance safety auditors, and other qualified persons may offer advice to strengthen programs. These experts also can provide fresh perspectives to improve a violence prevention program.

Workplace Security Analysis

The team or coordinator should periodically inspect the workplace and evaluate employee tasks to identify hazards, conditions, operations, and situations that could lead to violence. To find areas requiring further evaluation, the team or coordinator should do the following:

◆ Analyze incidents, including the characteristics of assailants and victims, an account of what happened before and during the incident, and the relevant details of the situation and its outcome. When possible, obtain police reports and recommendations.

◆ Identify jobs or locations with the greater risk of violence as well as processes and procedures that put employees at risk of assault, including how often and when.

◆ Note high-risk factors such as types of clients or patients (e.g., psychiatric conditions or patients disoriented by drugs, alcohol, or stress); physical risk factors of the building; isolated locations/job activities; lighting problems; lack of phones and other communication devices, areas of easy, unsecured access; and areas with previous security problems. (See sample checklist for assessing hazards in Appendix B.)

◆ Evaluate the effectiveness of existing security measures, including engineering control measures. Determine if risk factors have been reduced or eliminated, and take appropriate action.

Hazard Prevention and Control

Appendix B

After hazards of violence are identified through the systematic worksite analysis, the next step is to design measures through engineering or administrative work practices to prevent or control these hazards. If violence does occur, post-incidence response can be an important tool in preventing future incidents.

Engineering Controls and Workplace Adaptation

Engineering controls, for example, remove the hazard from the workplace or create a barrier between the worker and the hazard. There are several measures that can effectively prevent or control workplace hazards, such as those actions presented in the following paragraphs. The selection of any measure, of course, should be based upon the hazards identified in the workplace security analysis of each facility.

♦ Assess any plans for new construction or physical changes to the facility or workplace to eliminate or reduce security hazards.

♦ Install and regularly maintain alarm systems and other security devices, panic buttons, hand-held alarms or noise devices, cellular phones, and private channel radios where risk is apparent or may be anticipated, and arrange for a reliable response system when an alarm is triggered.

♦ Provide metal detectors – installed or hand-held, where appropriate – to identify guns, knives, or other weapons, according to the recommendations of security consultants.

♦ Use a closed-circuit video recording for high-risk areas on a 24-hour basis. Public safety is a greater concern than privacy in these situations.

♦ Place curved mirrors at hallway intersections or concealed areas.

♦ Enclose nurses' stations, and install deep service counters or bullet-resistant, shatter-proof glass in reception areas, triage, admitting, or client service rooms.

♦ Provide employee "safe rooms" for use during emergencies.

♦ Establish "time-out" or seclusion areas with high ceilings without grids for patients acting out and establish separate rooms for criminal patients.

♦ Provide client or patient waiting rooms designed to maximize comfort and minimize stress.

♦ Ensure that counseling or patient care rooms have two exits.

♦ Limit access to staff counseling rooms and treatment rooms controlled by using locked doors.

♦ Arrange furniture to prevent entrapment of staff. In interview rooms or crisis treatment areas, furniture should be minimal, lightweight, without sharp corners or edges, and/or affixed to the floor. Limit the number of pictures, vases, ashtrays, or other items that can be used as weapons.

♦ Provide lockable and secure bathrooms for staff members separate from patient-client, and visitor facilities.

♦ Lock all unused doors to limit access, in accordance with local fire codes.

♦ Install bright, effective lighting indoors and outdoors.

♦ Replace burned-out lights, broken windows, and locks.

♦ Keep automobiles, if used in the field, well-maintained. Always lock automobiles.

Administrative and Work Practice Controls

Administrative and work practice controls affect the way jobs or tasks are performed. The following examples illustrate how changes in work practices and administrative procedures can help prevent violent incidents.

♦ State clearly to patients, clients, and employees that violence is not permitted or tolerated.

♦ Establish liaison with local police and state prosecutors. Report all incidents of violence. Provide police with physical layouts of facilities to expedite investigations.

♦ Require employees to report all assaults or threats to a supervisor or manager (e.g., can be confidential interview). Keep logbooks and reports of such incidents to help in determining any necessary actions to prevent further occurrences.

◆ Advise and assist employees with, if needed, of company procedures for requesting police assistance in filing charges when assaulted.

◆ Provide management support during emergencies. Respond promptly to all complaints.

◆ Set up a trained response team to respond to emergencies.

◆ Use properly trained security officers, when necessary, to deal with aggressive behavior. Follow written security procedures.

◆ Ensure adequate and properly trained staff for restraining patients or clients.

◆ Provide sensitive and timely information to persons waiting in line or in waiting rooms. Adopt measures to decrease waiting time.

◆ Ensure adequate and qualified staff coverage at all times. Times of greatest risk occur during patient transfers, emergency responses, meal times, and at night. Locales with the greatest risk include admission units and crisis or acute care units. Other risks include admission of patients with a history of violent behavior or gang activity.

◆ Institute a sign-in procedure with passes for visitors, especially in a newborn nursery or pediatric department. Enforce visitor hours and procedures.

◆ Establish a list of "restricted visitors" for patients with a history of violence. Copies should be available at security checkpoints, nurses' stations, and visitor sign-in areas. Review and revise visitor check systems, when necessary. Limit information given to outsiders on hospitalized victims of violence.

◆ Supervise the movement of psychiatric clients and patients throughout the facility.

◆ Control access to facilities other than waiting rooms, particularly drug storage or pharmacy areas.

◆ Prohibit employees from working alone in emergency areas or walk-in clinics, particularly at night or when assistance is unavailable. Employees should never enter secluded rooms alone.

♦ Establish policies and procedures for secured areas, and emergency evacuations, and for monitoring high-risk patients at night (e.g., open versus locked seclusion).

♦ Ascertain the behavioral history of new and transferred patients to learn about any past violent or assaultive behaviors. Establish a system – such as chart tags, log books, or verbal census reports – to identify patients and clients with assaultive behavior problems, keeping in mind patient confidentiality and worker safety issues. Update as needed.

♦ Treat and/or interview aggressive or agitated clients in relatively open areas that still maintain privacy and confidentiality (e.g., rooms with removable partitions).

♦ Use case management conferences with co-workers and supervisors to discuss ways to effectively treat potentially violent patients.

♦ Prepare contingency plans to treat clients who are "acting out" or making verbal or physical attacks or threats. Consider using certified employee assistance professionals (CEAPs) or in-house social service or occupational health service staff to help diffuse patient or client anger.

♦ Transfer assaultive clients to "acute care units," "criminal units," or other more restrictive settings.

♦ Make sure that nurses and/or physicians are not alone when performing intimate physical examinations of patients.

♦ Discourage employees from wearing jewelry to help prevent possible strangulation in confrontational situations. Community workers should carry only required identification and money.

♦ Periodically survey the facility to remove tools or possessions left by visitors or maintenance staff, which could be used inappropriately by patients.

♦ Provide staff with identification badges, preferably without last names, to readily verify employment.

Appendix B

- ◆ Discourage employees from carrying keys, pens, or other items that could be used as weapons.
- ◆ Provide staff members with security escorts to parking areas in evening or late hours. Parking areas should be highly visible, well lighted, and safely accessible to the building.
- ◆ Use the "buddy system," especially when personal safety may be threatened. Encourage home health care providers, social service workers, and others to avoid threatening situations. Staff should exercise extra care in elevators, stairwells and unfamiliar residences; immediately leave premises if there is a hazardous situation; or request police escort if needed.
- ◆ Develop policies and procedures covering home health care providers, such as contracts on how visits will be conducted, the presence of others in the home during the visits, and the refusal to provide services in a clearly hazardous situation.
- ◆ Establish a daily work plan for field staff to keep a designated contact person informed about workers' whereabouts throughout the workday. If an employee does not report in, the contact person should follow up.
- ◆ Conduct a comprehensive post-incident evaluation, including psychological as well as medical treatment, for employees who have been subjected to abusive behavior.

Post-Incident Response

Post-incident response and evaluation are essential to an effective violence prevention program. All workplace violence programs should provide comprehensive treatment for victimized employees and employees who may be traumatized by witnessing a workplace violence incident. Injured staff should receive prompt treatment and psychological evaluation whenever an assault takes place, regardless of severity. (See sample hospital policy in Appendix C.) Transportation of the injured to medical care should be provided if care is not available on-site.

Victims of workplace violence suffer a variety of

consequences in addition to their actual physical injuries. These include short and long-term psychological trauma, fear of returning to work, changes in relationships with co-workers and family, feelings of incompetence, guilt, powerlessness, and fear of criticism by supervisors or managers. Consequently, a strong follow-up program for these employees will not only help them to deal with these problems, but also to help prepare them to confront or prevent future incidents of violence (Flannery, 1991, 1993, 1995).

There are several types of assistance that can be incorporated into the post-incident response. For example, trauma-crisis counseling, critical incident stress debriefing, or employee assistance programs may be provided to assist victims. Certified employee assistance professionals, psychologists, psychiatrists, clinical nurse specialists, or social workers could provide this counseling, or the employer can refer staff victims to an outside specialist. In addition, an employee counseling service, peer counseling, or support groups may be established.

In any case, counselors must be well trained and have a good understanding of the issues and consequences of assaults and other aggressive, violent behavior. Appropriate and promptly rendered post-incident debriefings and counseling reduce acute psychological trauma and general stress levels among victims and witnesses. In addition, such counseling educates staff about workplace violence and positively influences workplace and organizational cultural norms to reduce trauma associated with future incidents.

Training and Education
Training and education ensure that all staff are aware of potential security hazards and how to protect themselves and their co-workers through established policies and procedures.

Appendix B
All Employees

Every employee should understand the concept of "Universal Precautions for Violence," i.e., that violence should be expected but can be avoided or mitigated through preparation. Staff should be instructed to limit physical interventions in workplace altercations whenever possible, unless there are adequate numbers of staff or emergency response teams and security personnel available. Frequent training also can improve the likelihood of avoiding assault (Carmel and Hunter, 1990).

Employees who may face safety and security hazards should receive formal instructions on the specific hazards associated with the unit or job and facility. This includes information on the types of injuries or problems identified in the facility and the methods to control the specific hazards.

The training program should involve all employees, including supervisors and managers. New and reassigned employees should receive an initial orientation prior to being assigned their job duties. Visiting staff, such as physicians should receive the same training as permanent staff. Qualified trainers should instruct at the comprehensive level appropriate for the staff. Effective training programs should involve role-playing, simulations, and drills.

Topics may include Management of Assaultive Behavior; Professional Assault Response Training; police assault avoidance programs or personal safety training such as awareness, avoidance and how to prevent assaults. A combination of training may be used depending on the severity of the risk.

Required training should be provided to employees annually. In large institutions, refresher programs may be needed more frequently (monthly or quarterly) to effectively reach and inform all employees. The training should cover topics such as the following:

♦ The workplace violence prevention policy.

♦ Risk factors that cause or contribute to assaults.

♦ Early recognition of escalating behavior or recognition of warning signs or situations that may lead to assaults.

♦ Ways of preventing or diffusing volatile situations or aggressive behavior, managing anger, and appropriately using medications as chemical restraints.

♦ Information on multicultural diversity to develop sensitivity to racial and ethnic issues and differences.

♦ A standard response action plan for violent situations, including availability of assistance, response to alarm systems, and communicating procedures.

♦ How to deal with hostile persons other than patients and clients, such as relatives and visitors.

♦ Progressive behavior control methods and safe methods of restraint application or escape.

♦ The location and operation of safety devices such as alarm systems, along with the required maintenance schedules and procedures.

♦ Ways to protect oneself and coworkers, including use of the "buddy system."

♦ Policies and procedures for reporting and record keeping.

♦ Policies and procedures for obtaining medical care counseling, workers' compensation, or legal assistance after a violent episode or injury.

Supervisors, Managers, and Security Personnel

Supervisors and managers should ensure that employees are not placed in assignments that compromise safety and should encourage employees to report incidents. Employees and supervisors should be trained to behave compassionately towards

163

co-workers when an incident occurs.

Supervisors and managers should learn how to reduce security hazards and ensure that employees receive appropriate training. Following training, they should be able to recognize a potentially hazardous situation and to make any necessary changes in the physical plant, patient care treatment program, and staffing policy and procedures to reduce or eliminate the hazards.

Security personnel need specific training from the hospital or clinic, including the psychological components of handling aggressive and abusive clients, types of disorders, and ways to handle aggression and defuse hostile situations.
The training program should also include an evaluation. The content, methods, and frequency of training should be reviewed and evaluated annually by the team or coordinator responsible for implementation. Program evaluation may involve supervisor and/or employee interviews, testing and observing, and/or reviewing reports of behavior of individuals in threatening situations.

Recording Keeping and Evaluation of the Program
Record keeping and evaluation of the violence prevention program are necessary to determine overall effectiveness and identify any deficiencies or changes that should be made.

Record Keeping
Record keeping is essential to the success of a workplace violence prevention program. Good records help employers determine the severity of the problem, evaluate methods of hazard control, and identify training needs. Records can be especially useful to large organizations and for members of a business group or trade association who "pool" data. Records of injuries, illnesses, accidents, assaults, hazards, corrective actions, patient histories, and training, among others, can help identify problems

and solutions for an effective program. The following records are important:

♦ OSHA Log of Injury and Illness (OSHA 200). OSHA regulations require entry on the Injury and Illness Log of any injury that requires more than first aid, is a lost-time injury, requires modified duty, or causes loss of consciousness.[9] (This applies only to establishments required to keep OSHA logs.) Injuries caused by assaults, which are otherwise record able, also must be entered on the log. A fatality or catastrophe that results in the hospitalization of three or more employees must be reported to OSHA *within eight hours*. This includes those resulting from workplace violence and applies to *all* establishments.

♦ Medical reports of work injury and supervisors' reports for each recorded assault should be kept. These records should describe the type of assault, i.e., unprovoked sudden attack or patient-to-patient altercation; who was assaulted; and all other circumstances of the incident. The records should include a description of the environment or location, potential or actual cost, lost time, and the nature of injuries sustained.

♦ Incidents of abuse, verbal attacks or aggressive behavior – which may be threatening to the worker but do not result in injury, such as pushing or shouting and acts of aggression towards other clients – should be recorded, perhaps as part of an assaultive incident report. The affected department should evaluate these reports routinely. (See sample incident forms in Appendix D.)

♦ Information on patients with a history of past violence, drug abuse, or criminal activity should be recorded on the patient's chart. All staff who care for a potentially aggressive, abusive, or violent client should be aware of their background and history. Admission of violent clients should be logged to help determine potential risks.

♦ Minutes of safety meetings, records of hazard analyses, and

165

corrective actions recommended and taken should be documented.

♦ Records of all training programs, attendees, and qualifications of trainers should be maintained.

Evaluation

As part of their overall program, employers should evaluate their safety and security measures. Top management should review the program regularly, and with each incident, to evaluate program success. Responsible parties (managers, supervisors, and employees) should collectively reevaluate policies and procedures on a regular basis. Deficiencies should be identified and corrective action taken. An evaluation program should involve the following:

♦ Establishing a uniform violence reporting system and regular review of reports.

♦ Reviewing reports and minutes from staff meetings on safety and security issues.

♦ Analyzing trends and rates in illness/injury or fatalities caused by violence relative to   initial or "baseline" rates.

♦ Measuring improvement based on lowering the frequency and severity of workplace violence.

♦ Keeping up-to-date records of administrative and work practice changes to prevent workplace violence to evaluate their effectiveness.

♦ Surveying employees before and after making job or worksite changes or installing security measures or new systems to determine their effectiveness.

♦ Keeping abreast of new strategies available to deal with violence in the health care and social service fields as these develop.

♦ Surveying employees who experience hostile situations about the medical treatment they received initially and, again, several weeks afterward, and then several months later.

Notes

[5]According to a 1989 report (Wasserberger), 25 percent of major trauma patients treated in the emergency room carried weapons. Attacks in emergency rooms in gang-related shootings as well as planned escapes from police custody have been documented in hospitals. A 1991 report (Goetz et al.) also found that 17.3 percent of psychiatric patients searched were carrying weapons.

[6]OSHA's *Safety and Health Program Management Guidelines* (Fed. Reg. 54 (16):3904- 3916, January 26, 1989), provide for comprehensive safety and health programs containing these major elements. Employers with such programs can include workplace violence prevention efforts in that context.

[7]Title 29 U.S.C., Section 158(a) (2).

[8]Section 11(c)(1) of the OSH Act, which also applies to protected activity involving the hazard of workplace violence as it does for other health and safety matters: "No person shall discharge or in any manner discriminate against any employee because such employee has filed any complaint or instituted or caused to be instituted any proceeding under or related to this Act or has testified or is about to testify in any such proceeding or because of the exercise by such employee on behalf of himself or others of any right afforded by this Act."

[9]The Occupational Safety and Health Act and record keeping regulations in *Title 29 Code of Federal Regulations (CFR), Part 1904* provide specific recording requirements that comprise the framework of the occupational safety and health recording system (BLS, 1986a). BLS has issued guidelines that provide official Agency interpretations concerning the record keeping and reporting of occupational injuries and illnesses (BLS, 1986b).

APPENDIX C

WORKPLACE VIOLENCE

QUIZ ANSWERS

Workplace Violence Quiz Answers

1.   There is no need to worry about workplace violence be cause the number of reported homicides at work is de creasing. **False**.

Although the number of work-related homicides has decreased in the last several years, incidents, which have not resulted in death but have produced physical or psychological injury, have been on the rise. Workplace assaults and vio lent acts continue to be a significant problem facing employers today.

2.   All verbal threats should be reported and investigated since this is a form of violence. **True**.

Verbal threats are a form of workplace violence, and are also sometimes the first clue that something is not right with an employee. Verbal threats very often precede acts of workplace violence, and should be taken very seriously.

3. Internal violence usually comes from customers, vendors and members of the public. **False.**

> Internal violence comes from current and former employees, and in situations in which domestic violence occurs in the workplace, even if the spouse or partner of the employee involved is not employed with the organization.

4. There is no way to tell if someone has the potential to become violent. **False.**

> Although the prediction of violence is not a perfect science, odds improve when we are able to assess the risk factors that are associated with higher rates of violence. Thus, although we cannot predict absolutely who will and will not act in a violent manner, we can assess level of risk for acting out aggressively and intervene accordingly.

5. All employees who have verbalized threats should be terminated immediately. **False.**

> All reported threats need to be first investigated, and then, based upon the information gathered during the investigation, decisions can be made as to how to intervene most appropriately (i.e., termination, suspension or other disciplinary action, fitness-for-duty exam, etc.)

6. Employee Assistance Programs (EAP) can be useful in preventing workplace violence. **True**

> Employee Assistance Programs can be very effective in offering assistance to those employees who are having emotional or psychological difficulties. These programs also typically offer a management consultation service, so that

supervisors can call the EAP with their concerns
and obtain guidance on how to intervene with
problem employees. If employees are offered
options other than violence at an early stage, such
as treatment or organizational intervention, they
may be less prone to resort to extreme actions such
as threats and aggression.

7.   When an incident of workplace violence occurs, the
responsibility for the incident lies with the individual, and
not with the organization itself. **False.**

While the responsibility for one's actions
ultimately rests with the perpetrator of any violent
act, organizations also have a responsibility to set
up appropriate policies and procedures for
identifying and intervening with at-risk
employees. Additionally, there are organizational
risk factors, relating to how companies are
organized and managed, that may increase the
likelihood that a violent incident would occur. All
organizations need to be responsible for doing
what they can to create a safe working
environment.

8.   Effective pre-employment screening, including the use
of background checks on new employees, can effectively
reduce violence. **True.**

The use of pre-employment screening, reference
checks and background investigations can alert a
potential new employer to any risk factors which
may suggest a propensity for aggression and
violence, thus allowing an employer to avoid
hiring an individual who may present a safety risk
further down the road. Organizations should check
with their legal counsel before using any pre-hire

screening process to determine whether there are any legal issues pertaining to the use of these processes in the area of the country in which they are located.

9. The purpose of a Threat Assessment Team is to determine whether or not an individual will commit an act of violence. **False**.

No one individual or team of people can determine absolutely whether an individual will or will not become violent. The purpose of the Threat Assessment Team is to gather as much information as possible about the individual who has allegedly made the threat and the situation, determine possible appropriate interventions for the individual and the organization, choose and implement a plan of action, and monitor the situation for any escalation or changes. In cases where a violent incident has already occurred, the Threat Assessment Team will mobilize counseling and security resources, assist affected employees in obtaining medical and insurance benefits, and provide updates and information to managers and other employees.

10. A Fitness-for-duty evaluation can be done by any licensed medical or mental health professional. **True.**

Technically, this is a true statement. However, for assessing potential violence in the workplace, we recommend that organizations interview various medical and psychological providers and identify those who have experience specifically in the area of workplace violence and threat assessment. We also recommend that organizations utilize providers who have some expertise with how organizations and businesses function, so that recommendations are relevant and pertinent to the workplace.

11. Training staff, supervisors and managers is one of the less effective methods of implementing a violence prevention program in an organization. **False**

The training of managers and employees can actually be one of the most effective methods of reducing threats and violence in the workplace. When individuals are taught to recognize the early warning signs of a potential problem, and are instructed about where to report threats and policy violations, intervention with troubled employees can occur much earlier.

12. Security systems tend not to be very effective in situa tions where the person making the threat is an em ployee, because the employee typically has access to the facility anyway. **False.**

Security systems, when used effectively, can monitor who enters and leaves a facility, and can restrict access to those who do not have a "key card" or other clearance to enter the facil ity. Additionally, the use of "panic buttons" and video cameras can alert those within an organi zation about a problem as it is occurring.

13. Workplace Violence policies should include a statement about "limited tolerance." **False.**

Workplace violence policies should emphasize zero tolerance of threats and threatening actions, weapons on the organization's property, and aggressive and violent actions.

14.   An employer cannot get into trouble for keeping an
       employee that they suspect may be capable of violence.
       False.

       An employer can be held liable if they were aware
       of threats, threatening action, previous violence
       and/or concern on the part of other employees and
       failed to act on that information to ensure a safe
       workplace.

15.   Type II violence includes domestic violence incidents.
       False.

       Type II events include those which occur at the
       hands of someone who is the object or recipient
       of a service of the business that is affected. Type
       III violence is related to an employment
       relationship with the organization, and includes
       domestic violence., while Type I violence occurs
       during the commission of a crime (i.e., robbery).

About The Authors

S. Anthony Baron, Ph.D., Psy.D.

Author, speaker and recognized pioneer in workplace violence prevention, Dr. Anthony Baron has been described as "America's leading researcher into workplace violence" and the "most accurate" profiler by a recent definitive study of workplace violence entitled *New Arenas for Violence*. Working with clients in all areas of the public and private sectors, Dr. Baron has also been retained by the United States Postal Service to provide workplace violence and threat assessment training throughout the United States. He served on an Executive Committee for the Postal Service in Washington, D.C., which has implemented training based on his book for over 750,000 postal personnel.

Dr. Baron was selected to be a keynote speaker for the only two Cal/OSHA Conferences on workplace safety and security. A dynamic and effective communicator, who combines sensitivity with practical information, Dr. Baron was recognized by the Federal Executive Board and the city of Oklahoma City for his post-trauma work after the bombing of the federal building there. Dr. Baron is the only person in the country who has served as an expert consultant and trainer for the United States Postal Service, the Oklahoma City bombing incident, and OSHA. His client list includes many Fortune 100 companies, leading universities and hospitals. Dr. Baron also has served as a consultant to the International Association of Police Chiefs, CNN, USA Today, The Wall Street Journal, Newsweek, and 48 Hours.

Dr. Baron is the author of the first book in the country on workplace violence entitled, *Violence in the Workplace: A Prevention and Management Guide for Businesses*, considered by many corporate leaders as mandatory reading. His second book is entitled, *Violence in Our Schools, Hospitals, and Public Places*. An active author on career transition, change management, downsizing and emotional issues surrounding life and work performance, Dr. Baron is an author of several workbooks and has been published in national business journals, leading national newspapers, and major publications.

Dr. Baron is featured in several highly acclaimed and award-winning video and audio training series including *Dying to Work* and *Violence in the Workplace: From Prevention to Intervention*. An Honors graduate of Biola University and the United States International University, Dr. Baron holds graduate degrees in Psychology, Marriage & Family Therapy, and Organizational Development and has completed post-doctoral continuing education work at Harvard Medical School.

Dr. Baron is a member of the American Psychological Association, the California Psychological Association, and the Society of Human Resources Management. He has been awarded Diplomate of the American Board of Forensic Examiners, Diplomate of the American Board of Psychological Specialties, Diplomate of the American Board of Forensic Medicine, and Board Certified and Fellow of the American Academy of Experts in Traumatic Stress.

Suzanne Hoffman, Ph.D.

Suzanne Hoffman, Ph.D. is a licensed psychologist (PSY15000) and organizational consultant who has specialized in the areas of Workplace Violence Prevention and Intervention, Violence Risk Assessment, Critical Incident Debriefing, and Workplace Sexual Harassment. Dr. Hoffman's professional expertise includes consulting with a variety of organizations regarding difficult and potentially dangerous employees. Additionally, she has conducted Fitness-for-duty Evaluations with employees who have exhibited a variety of emotional difficulties in the workplace. As a corporate consultant, Dr. Hoffman has also utilized her training and experience from both the clinical and the organizational milieus to assist companies in intervening with employees and executives who have engaged in sexually harassing behavior. Dr. Hoffman has also developed a unique individualized sexual harassment intervention program, created as an alternative to group training for managers and executives, which emphasizes education, insight and behavioral change. Her experience includes post-trauma counseling and critical incident debriefing in organizations which have experienced incidents of workplace violence and other workplace tragedies. Dr. Hoffman has worked with individuals from a variety of cultural and diagnostic backgrounds, and has interfaced with Human Resources and Management teams to assist in the implementation of Sexual Harassment and Workplace Violence policies and procedures.

As Executive Vice President of Baron Center, Inc., Dr. Hoffman oversees a staff of trainers and psychologists. In addition to providing consulting and psychological services, she conducts seminars on Sexual Harassment and Workplace Violence Prevention and Intervention from both an individual and an organizational perspective. Recognized as a sensitive and effective speaker, Dr. Hoffman offers practical direction to Human Resource and Management professionals. Additionally, she provides pragmatic suggestions for dealing with inappropriate, emotionally enraged and potentially dangerous employees. Dr. Hoffman also provides insight into effective pre-employment screening and hiring practices, which can assist in identifying the potential problem employee during the application process.

Dr. Hoffman holds an undergraduate degree in psychology

from San Diego State University, and earned both a Master's degree and a Doctorate in Clinical Psychology from the California School of Professional Psychology in San Diego. A member of both the American Psychological Association (APA) and the San Diego Psychological Association (SDPA), Dr. Hoffman currently serves as the co-chair of the Women's Issues Committee for SDPA. Dr. Hoffman is also a member of the Employee Assistance Program Association (EAPA) and The American College of Forensic Examiners. Other areas of expertise include psychological testing and evaluation, stress management, women's transition issues and domestic violence in the workplace.

James G. Merrill

James G. Merrill is a human resources executive with over 25 years of experience in the private and public sectors. As a Human Resource executive working within the U.S. Postal Service, he was responsible for addressing issues related to workplace violence. Specifically, Mr. Merrill investigated a number of violent incidents, assessed potentially violent employees, and designed and implemented systems, protocols and training to reduce the threat of violence within the Postal system.

Mr. Merrill has written various articles on the subject of workplace violence, and was featured in the Personnel Journal. Additionally, he has conducted numerous seminars nationally on the subject of maintaining a non-violent workplace. Mr. Merrill has provided various types of training to Threat Assessment Teams in many organizations, including Symantac, the U.S. Postal Service, Bay Area Rapid Transit, Sony, Office of Personnel Management, Department of the Army, San Jose State Professional Development Center, various Society for Human Resource Management Chapters and the American Management Association.

The Authors

In addition to being a human resources executive, Mr. Merrill is currently a member of the faculty for San Jose State University, and has previously served as an adjunct professor at Cornell University. Mr. Merrill is also a current member and past president for the Santa Clara Chapter of the Society for Human Resource Management and is a current Board member for the Northern California Human Resource Association. He also serves as a member of the Advisory Board for the San Jose State University Human Resources Certificate Program, and is a Bay Area Human Resources Executive Council Member.

Mr. Merrill continues to consult on Workplace Violence Prevention issues and can be contacted at jimgiants@aol.com.

About Baron Center, Inc.

Baron Center, Inc. is a worldwide leader in providing workplace violence and school violence intervention, prevention and protection programs. Baron Center, Inc. provides a wide range of resources for hospitals, universities, corporations and government agencies that are interested in providing a safe working environment including:

Workplace Violence Prevention Training
Threat Assessment Team Training
Training Videos
Risk Assessment
Sexual Harassment Training
Speaking Engagements
and
Over twenty workbooks authored by Drs. Anthony Baron and Suzanne Hoffman

Visit Our Website:
www.baroncenter.com

(800)391-4267

Index

A

B

C

D

Index

Index